To Gladys —
Thanks for always
being there.

[signature]
9/15/93

MEMOS FR~~OM~~ **To** MANAGEMENT

MEMOS FR~~OM~~ *To* MANAGEMENT

There's Nothing Wrong With Serving A Lousy Cup of Coffee if ...

Michael H. Mescon, Ph.D.
Timothy S. Mescon, Ph.D.
and Susan Harte

LONGSTREET PRESS
Atlanta, Georgia

Published by LONGSTREET PRESS, INC.,
a subsidiary of Cox Newspapers,
a division of Cox Enterprises, Inc.
2140 Newmarket Parkway
Suite 118
Marietta, Georgia 30067

Printed in the United States of America

1st printing, 1993

Library of Congress Catalog Number 92-84007

ISBN: 1-56352-066-4

This book was printed by R.R. Donnelley & Sons, Harrisonburg,
Virginia.

Jacket design by Jill Dible / Illustration by Laurie Shock
Book design by Laura McDonald

DEDICATION

To all those who "wished I had
said that." Now you can.
Enjoy!

— INTRODUCTION —

This book may not be another *War and Peace*, but it does deal with something that touches nearly all of us every day of our adult lives — organizational war and peace. Regrettably, surveys of people who work for pay tend to suggest that there is more of the former than of the latter. In an effort to address the behaviors and attitudes — from manager to clerk — that create an organization's cultural ambience, we give you a collection, a potpourri, of vignettes in memo form.

We selected this format for you to use seriously or in jest, in the event you would like to share the memos with people you think could find benefit or amusement in them. You can tear them out and send them to those you wish well — or not so well. Although in an ideal world compatriots would be able to converse with each other openly and respectfully, the corporate setting presents such an ideal only infrequently. We offer you, then, some ways to make points you might like to make, but for one reason or another cannot. If we've done a good job, you will be able to do one or all of the following:

- Say, "I knew that already."
- Say, "I wish my boss/colleague knew that."
- Say, "He or she will know it after reading this memo."

You might wonder, what gives Mike, Tim and Susan

credibility in an era when all someone need do to be regarded as an expert is to proclaim himself or herself one? It is this. We are all working stiffs, and have been for many years. Although everyone has to report to someone, somehow — and each of us has management experience — we currently run the gamut. Mike has spent most of his career being a manager. Tim's worklife has been a combination of managee and manager. Susan claims to have vast knowledge of what it's like to be managed.

Essentially, we are dealing with simple truths, common sense and routine occurrences that we have noted as part of our education in vocational life. If you have not experienced — or suffered, as the case may be — the same things, perhaps you haven't lived long enough or worked in settings that are business-as-usual for most people. In any event, we hope you'll find a use for some of our memos. At the very least, we hope they will give rise to a few knowing smiles.

MEMORANDUM

TO:

FROM:

RE: LAGNIAPPE

Imagine this if you will: You are sitting in a high school auditorium on the rural eastern shore of Maryland. At exactly 8:00 p.m., octogenarian Lionel Hampton — leading a troupe of twenty people, all much younger then he — steps on stage. At 8:01 p.m., the band begins to play. Hampton, as you know, is one of the world's great xylophonists. For decades he has entertained audiences throughout the world. He is a musician, conductor and writer.

He is also a manager.

What he gave that audience that night in that sleepy town was no less than what he has given to audiences globally for more than sixty years. The Cajuns have a word for the treatment. Mr. Hampton and company gave their customers "lagniappe," which means "a little bit more, a little bit extra." You see, Lionel Hampton understands that it is this treatment, coupled with solid talent and a great supporting cast, that has separated him from everyone else in a hypercompetitive marketplace. Giving lagniappe at each and every opportunity distinguishes the world-class from the no-class, the winner from the runner-up.

That Maryland audience probably would have been content with a one-hour performance of mediocre content, coupled with the chance to visit with this musical legend. What it got instead was a nonstop, four-hour concert that concluded with Mr. Hampton's leading his band (i.e., organization) through the audience and onto the street to the strains of "When the Saints Go Marchin' In." This was lagniappe at work. It's just a little bit more, a little bit extra, and it is what always separates the memorable from the mundane in the public's mind.

MEMORANDUM

TO:

FROM:

**RE: BELIEVE WHAT I SAY.
IGNORE WHAT I DO.**

Consider for a moment a company we'll call Amalgamated Amalgamation. It's an old company, proud of its tired heritage and still haplessly bound to doing things the way they've always been done. In fact, dear old Amalgamated Amalgamation is so entrenched in its own sense of righteousness that it manages to take the most modern ideas, grind them through interminable meetings, and emerge pleased with itself — for keeping comfortable that which others find intensely uncomfortable.

Because the amalgamated products industry, along with numerous others, began facing diminished profitability about the time the employee empowerment philosophies took hold in the late 1980s, Amalgamated got scared and hired some consultants. One of them devised, administered and quantified an employee survey.

When the results were presented, Amalgamated executives were genuinely shocked to learn that the workforce was, in the main, hostile, frustrated and mistrustful of a management it regarded as ignorant, insensitive and arrogant. "You don't have a clue about the heart of this organization and the potential that resides here," the message seemed to read, "and furthermore, you don't give a rat's behind as long as the cash registers ring."

Management wrung its hands and sent out a memo. It said, in effect, "Gee, we're shocked and embarrassed and distressed to learn that you perceive us this way. We're actually very informed, sensitive and humble people. We know we need you. We value you. We're going to address your concerns. Just wait and see."

And sure enough, there were some statements about free and open communication — you know, employee empowerment stuff. There was diplomacy school for middle managers and, for the rank and file, opportunities to expand horizons — until budget constraints precluded them. There were rah-rah, hyperbolic memos from various department heads posted on various bulletin boards.

But there was not another take-the-pulse survey of the entire employee body, nothing to measure changed — or unchanged — attitudes.

Well.

Time has passed. Were dear old Amalgamated Amalgamation to do such a follow-up survey now, it would probably learn that its employees still feared management and still regarded it as ignorant, insensitive and arrogant. The only change would be that the rank and file now also viewed top brass as just plain stupid.

MEMORANDUM

TO:

FROM:

RE: THE ROMANCE OF LEADERSHIP

While you'd not venture so far as to claim a resemblance between Lee Iacocca and Errol Flynn, or between John Watson and Charlton Heston, there is a certain *je ne sais quois* about some business people that separates the pacesetters from the merely talented. At the core of the most intriguing of these individuals, there is an elusive something we'll call "romanticism."

■ It's mischievous. It's a certain kind of wit that enables them to make a joke or take one.

■ It's irreverent. While this trait makes the pious cringe and the uptight choke, it says to real people, "Hey, we're not talking here about the monumental struggles of humankind — we're just making widgets."

■ It's mesmerizing. Whereas great tyrants are merely peculiar, memorable leaders are exotic.

■ It's infectious. There's a benevolent madness about great executives. They are composed enough to reveal a fanciful bent and disciplined enough to focus it. These people electrify their organizations.

Unless, that is, their romanticism is snuffed out somewhere along the way. Companies that frown upon romanticism end up with lethargy where there should be energy.

MEMORANDUM

TO:

FROM:

RE: GETTING WELL TOGETHER

The late Robert Woodruff, of Coca-Cola fame, set out to build a great organization. When pressed for a definition of a great organization, Mr. Woodruff said that it was a business where "everyone got well together." When Woodruff said everyone, he meant it. Owners, staff members, customers, vendors, and the potpourri of Coke constituencies were all part of Woodruff's "get-well" family. In actuality, this get-well concept is a hallmark of gold-medal-winning endeavors. It often separates the winners from the also-rans, the champions from the pretenders.

MEMORANDUM

TO:

FROM:

RE: ON LOYALTY

Statesman George F. Kenan once dryly noted that, in politics, "loyalty is the only absolute human value."

American executives have of late been bewailing the dearth of employee loyalty. When they do so, they seem to forget that, eternally in politics and traditionally in business, "loyalty" really means mindless acquiescence to a party line, a my-side-right-or-wrong kind of thing. Some even take this attitude to the extreme by saying to an employee — as did recently the president of Amalgamated Amalgamation's commercial real estate operation — "I demand your loyalty."

What this unfortunate gentleman seems to have forgotten is that loyalty, like love, is earned. And like love, it works best when given spontaneously. To demand it is not only a contradiction in logic, but also is likely to engender disloyalty instead. Now, the flipside.

Imagine this. You're in a food store in Norwalk, Connecticut. Within fifteen miles of this food store there are a hundred others. The food store you're in stocks fewer than 1,000 items. The average grocery might stock 15,000 to 20,000 items. The nerve center of the store is a milk-processing plant. Why are you there?

The answer provides a post-graduate education in making the uncommon common. You are standing in the only aisle (in order to encourage impulse buying) at Stew Leonard's World Famous Dairy Store. Last week, shopping at Stew Leonard's was something akin to a Hawaiian vacation. An hour from New York City and near nothing else in particular, Stew Leonard's is a retailer's fondest dream. Sixty-year-old Stew Leonard, Stew Jr. and family have written the book on transforming the most mundane of experiences into one of the most fun. And at Stew Leonard's, business is fun for all.

In a given year, 2.5 million customers visit Stew Leonard's store, providing, by far, the highest sales per square foot ($2,700) in the industry. The dairy, the store's original business, sells 10 million quarts of milk each year. Only now, after decades of perfecting perfection, is Stew Leonard constructing a second store in Danbury, Connecticut. Making the uncommon common has made this store an exemplar of what's good and right with business. Thousands of customers come back weekly to buy world-class products from a world-class retailer. A simple business doing simply splendidly.

World-class organizations love and respect staff members, who in turn not only reciprocate, but transmit the same to each and every customer. Everyone prospers, and this prosperity is the magic of world class. World-class enterprises, big or small, public or private, concentrate on making the uncommon common by making good things happen to good people both inside and outside the organization.

This is loyalty in action.

MEMORANDUM

TO:

FROM:

RE: THE OSMOSIS OF FEAR

Fear is born in childhood, the offspring of our system of socializing the young and setting examples for them. Sadly, corporate cultures merely continue the process by adding to it an undue regard for status, money and power at the expense of honor and substance. There are dozens of places in which vocational fear is spawned — sales quotas and performance evaluations intended to stave off discrimination lawsuits rather than to assess growth. Fear is unduly generated by superfluous authority, by the prideful hiding of ignorance, by allowing people to compensate for insecurity rather than overcome it, and by a tenacious belief that people won't work unless someone pummels them.

MEMORANDUM

TO:

FROM:

RE: WHAT'S THE BIG SECRET?

Whispers in the halls. Innuendo at meetings. Sly comments by the water fountain. Mysterious e-mail memoranda. What's it all about? At all too many organizations, there is a control of information that is devastating, destructive and downright insulting. Obviously, when legally protected securities information or legal issues are involved, circumspection is warranted. But how often is information hoarded, just because? Because of a need to control, a need for power, a need for one-upsmanship, a need to tease, a need to assert one's position inappropriately. How often do we truly respond to the age-old question, "What's the big secret?" More damage is done by suppressing information than by sharing it with professionals who might (God forbid!) enhance the decision-making process.

Incubating ill will and suspicion is simply an unhealthy act, counterproductive to the mission of any enterprise. Share, and you will find bright, ambitious professionals with unique insights into solving complicated and difficult problems. Do yourself a favor. Let the cat out of the bag.

MEMORANDUM

TO:

FROM:

**RE: THERE IS NO SUCH THING
AS A COMMODITY**

What is a commodity? In days gone by, one might have mentioned bread, milk, butter and a host of other agricultural staples that could be transported and distributed. Today, few products and services are *not* perceived to be commodities. Financial, accounting, legal and medical services are often categorized as such. After all, can you differentiate one certificate of deposit, one will or one tonsillectomy from another, any more than you can tell one baking potato from another? Standardized tax filings and wills are now more the rule than the exception. And shoes, shirts and computers can be called commodities because they are considered to be both interchangeable and replaceable.

But Harvard Business School Professor Theodore Leavitt argues that there is no such thing as a "commodity."

Why not? Because each of us, in our own enterprise, in our own way, has the opportunity and the challenge to differentiate our products and services from all others in the marketplace.

If it's possible to develop quality, competitive products, then the challenge is in distinguishing your quality, competitive products from everything else that's similar. If there is no difference, why would anyone choose to do business with you?

MEMORANDUM

TO:

FROM:

RE: YOU CAN'T BE SERIOUS.

"People take this too seriously," says the manager, upon confronting a worker's distress over an annual review.

If it's not to be taken seriously, then why do it?

MEMORANDUM

TO:

FROM:

**RE: THE THREE MOST ADMIRED
CHARACTERISTICS**

A recent survey of some 2,000 people by ad agency D'Arcy Masius Benton & Bowles, Inc., delivers an important message to managers at all levels. Three of the characteristics most admired in others were warmth, sense of humor and honesty. Isn't this what most of us want?

What most of us get however, is all too often quite the contrary. This is the bad news.

The good news is that warmth, humor, honesty and compassion are not genetically transferred traits. They are, in fact, carefully developed characteristics fortified by organizations committed to the importance of the "touch factor" in buying and selling. We are so surprised when we find ourselves confronted by one or all of these factors that we often go out of our way to buy and buy again. The touch factor reduces customer sensitivity to price and enhances the customer's desire to see the salesperson make a sale. Imagine letting customers work for you and your organization. Picture them leaving your business and proclaiming to the world that their last transaction approached the pleasures of a Club Med holiday.

MEMORANDUM

TO:

FROM:

RE: REVOLTING TIME

When things get revolting, perhaps it's time to revolt.

In 1976, British management consultant Robert
Marsh wrote that the time had come for radical
changes in the management of organizations. While
declaring that managers must be the change agents,
he warned that the process of making alterations on
others — whether they be people or systems — com-
pels us to alter the way we do business. This was
great advice in 1976. In 1996, it will probably still be
being preached interminably in text and seminar. Will
anyone listen? We hope so. Are many listening now,
when "management" and "leadership" are already
national preoccupations? We think not.

Some executives appear to be listening, while count-
less experts talk and exhort, but few appear to be
implementing. It is almost as if the mere fact of hear-
ing and agreeing represent a proper substitute for
doing what needs to be done. This is akin to recognizing the dangers of smoking, but failing to realize
that they apply to you.

Take the case of a major furniture retailer. Five million in furniture sold and one million returned. From
a dollar perspective, twenty percent of everything

that went out came back in. It was more like a revolving door than a sales transaction.

In attempting to find out why, management talked with the salespeople and was assured the problem resided in warehousing and delivery. Management then talked to personnel in those areas and was informed in no uncertain terms that the blame rested with the salespeople.

At this point, you have the not-so-unusual situation of one segment of an organization attempting to build its status on the ruins of another. When back-stabbing becomes the primary endeavor of a business, everyone loses.

After examining the return problem with those who sold and those who delivered, it was recommended by a company maverick that it might be wise to talk to those returning the merchandise. Specifically, she suggested listening to the consumer.

The results were both interesting and beneficial. According to customers, over 89 percent of the returns originated on the sales floor and were generated by lack of product knowledge coupled with a failure to comprehend customer needs. For example, a 100-inch sofa simply won't do for an 89-inch wall. It may be purchased, but it will come back.

By listening, the company pinpointed the true causes of customer dissatisfaction and — with the help of sales, warehouse and delivery personnel — developed solutions that effectively treated the problem.

MEMORANDUM

TO:

FROM:

**RE: LITTLE THINGS
    MEAN EVERYTHING**

"Why me?"

How often do consumers raise this cry? How often do the buyers of the world proclaim to its sellers that they have been abused, humiliated and humbled yet one more time?

Mind you, it isn't the major catastrophes that disenchant and dishearten. It's the aggregate of the little things that makes the difference between satisfaction and indignation. It is what happens during the entire buying and selling transaction. Consumers remember all that takes place from the moment they enter the store to the instant they leave, and that total experience, in fact, determines whether they will ever return.

Too many sellers simply forget that the little things are killers. They kill customer satisfaction, which kills customer loyalty, which kills sellers.

It was obviously the customer's fault. It was, without question, according to the counter worker of one of the largest vendors of ice cream in the world, the sole and solitary error of the customer. The shouting could be heard for miles. The result was unhappiness, dissatisfaction, and another sterling example of clerks moving in swiftly for the kill.

The scenario was a little girl's first birthday. Mom and Dad were to pick up an ice cream cake and deliver it to the day-care center, where all the children would celebrate this momentous occasion. The couple had gone to the store a week in advance in order to pick out the perfect cake for their perfect baby.

After thirty minutes of careful study, they selected a cake and gave careful instructions: "Please put 'Happy Birthday, Abbie!' on the cake." The counter person, wearing the name of that store emblazoned on her chest, said, "Happy Birthday, Abbie!" The couple said, "That's A-B-B-I-E. Shall we write it down?" The clerk said, "Of course not!"

Fatal error. Day of celebration arrives, Mom and Dad are running late, rush to pick up special surprise, and cake reads, "Happy Birthday, Abdie!" Script was beautifully done, cake looked delicious, but neither parent knew a child named A-B-D-I-E. The harassed parents explained the error to the company's front-line representative, who informed them that clearly, a week earlier, they had said "D," not "B." She was moving in for the kill. The parents politely explained that for a year now they were certain of the spelling of their daughter's name and would appreciate a quick resolution of the problem. The clerk said, "It will cost you." What she didn't understand was that while the customers were being executed, so, too, were the earnings of the business. Cause and effect is simple, isn't it?

MEMORANDUM

TO:

FROM:

RE: TRUE PARTICIPATION: NOT EASY

Despotic management feeds on compliance and obedience. It's the yours-is-not-to-reason-why approach to goal attainment. For many, such despotism is actually comforting, since it eliminates the need for conscious thought and rational decision making. In essence, the do-what-you're-told-and-you-will-be-cared-for philosophy reduces us to prison inmates or animals in a zoo. We may be sacrificing our birthright for the proverbial mess of pottage.

Transfer this truth to running a business. Few would argue for closed, rigid, authoritarian structures. Certainly not in this country. It's just not the "American Way." On the other hand, don't make the uncritical assumption that all would opt for that endeavor where true and complete participation is the order of the day.

What we're trying to say is true participation means just that. True participation better mean all for one and one for all. True participation should imply we'll either get sick together or well together. True participation means I am willing to take complete responsibility for my contributions or lack thereof. True participation does not signify survival of the fittest, but rather a nurturing climate where we truly wish one another well. True participation shuns scapegoating and places a premium upon deliverables and accountability. True participation is damn tough and demands the best and highest from each person.

In effect, true participation is a continuous process. It fosters a unique culture with its own set of folkways, mores, institutional ways and taboos. In action, true participation will take your breath away. True participation isn't easy. Why should it be?

MEMORANDUM

TO:

FROM:

RE: IN LOCO PARENTIS

You think there's no fear in your organization just because management is composed of nice people painstakingly trained to observe the Ten Commandments?

Think again. Fear isn't manifested only in people who wilt in the presence of authority figures, or who are too timid to make a decision. Fear is right there whenever there's resistance to change, passive and active retaliation, short-term and self-serving thinking, and obsession with control.

Whoever feels fear imposes it, effectively dampening communication and candor.

Among the rank and file, assertiveness inhibited nurtures bitterness, sneakiness and cowardice. Among managers, it leads inevitably to the mindless, conform-or-perish mentality that is just as prevalent among nervous MBAs as it is among floor supervisors who barely made it out of eighth grade.

Fear promotes immaturity and self-preoccupation — and silence — at a time when the nation needs boldness and cooperation.

You think that fearful people are too fully formed now, in adulthood, for any interference in the syndrome to be meaningful? That it's a job for religious leaders and psychological counselors? That you've got enough to do running a business without playing therapist to a stupefying number of personality problems?

That's fair — an organization built for productivity of goods or services shouldn't have to be more than that — but unfortunately, it's not true. It's not true because of the mere fact that in today's world, people spend more waking hours at work than they do anywhere else. They have more daily interactions with coworkers than with families.

Therefore, dealing with fear becomes — by default — a task for the corporation. In loco parentis, if you will.

MEMORANDUM

TO:

FROM:

RE: IT NEVER ENDS

If you plan to stay in the race, don't expect it to ever end, because it won't. You will need to pay your dues every day, and that payment only entitles you to get in line to pay again the next day. This is what it takes to be competitive and profitable. It is not an easy life, for a company or for an individual.

While ordinary companies — and ordinary people — strive to keep their constituents satisfied, the world class intend to give you more.

There is a cute television commercial starring Garfield the Cat, where the fetching feline quips, "Don't change a thing." In this vignette, Garfield is a hotel customer and is truly pleased. Consumers who feel this way become good customers and good salespeople for the pleasing organization. Interestingly enough, pleasing organizations have always been more concerned with customers than competition. The reality is, if you please your customers, you don't have to spend valuable time knocking your competitors . . . your customers will assume this unique responsibility.

This is why pleasing organizations are usually world-class profit-makers. They consistently spend their time, energy, and money on product/service improvement and delivery rather than on bullying and bashing others.

Admittedly, having customers tell you "Don't change a thing" is an admirable goal. However, attaining it is dependent upon leadership which recognizes that satisfied customers result from a continually improving organization where change becomes the status quo.

MEMORANDUM

TO:

FROM:

**RE: IF TWO PEOPLE SAY
YOU'RE DRUNK, LIE DOWN**

We always liked the admonition, "If two people say
you're drunk, lie down." Even if you don't drink, they
think you do, and it would be smart to find out why.

Undoubtedly, an understanding of self provides you
with a monumental edge in understanding others.
The best, most secure executives comprehend their
strengths and weaknesses and, by doing so, constantly improve. Knowing how you are perceived by
others is basic, if sometimes painful. For example,
have you ever listened to yourself on a recorder and
suddenly realized that, instead of having the tonal
quality of the late Orson Wells, you sound more like
Gomer Pyle?

In short, don't be afraid to lie down if necessary. You
might find the rest does you good.

MEMORANDUM

TO:

FROM:

**RE: SPARE US YOUR
    SELF-IMPORTANCE**

For pity's sake, if you have something to say to someone in confidence, say it behind closed doors. Don't
draw him or her into a corner or, worse, stand in the
middle of a roomful of people and whisper.

Such behavior not only announces your deplorable
manners, but also tells the world that your fondness
for self-importance exceeds your good sense.

What do people do when they see others whispering?
Even the most devoutly non-nosey will strain their
ears to hear. Is that what you're really after?

MEMORANDUM

TO:

FROM:

**RE: YOU CAN'T YELL THINGS
INTO PLACE**

This is brutal, but hit me some more, OK?

Tyranny wears many faces that appear in all kinds of companies. It can be overtly threatening, stern and bellicose. It can appear to be friendly, understanding and supportive. Whatever the mask, though, its overriding aim is to produce compliance and obedience. Things are ordered into place, and — regardless of outward appearances — there is little room for deviation from those orders. There's no such thing as "Inform me of what needs to be done, and then leave me alone while I do it."

Some people rail against tyranny. They either find their way to other workplaces or stay, allowing themselves to become defeated and soured.

Other people, however, outwardly whine about their bondage while inwardly finding comfort in it. Assuming the guise of martyrs, some even sullenly convince themselves that they're earning Brownie points for the privilege. While few employees would embrace tyranny, the urge to gripe and moan about closed, rigid, authoritarian structures has become institutionalized. These people wouldn't know what to do with true and complete participation because, frankly, it requires too much of them. They're accustomed to being restrained, belittled or abused, and when that's gone, they miss it. They are the people who make sure that, within a corporate structure, there's always room for a tyrant.

MEMORANDUM

TO:

FROM:

**RE: DO ONE THOUSAND THINGS
ONE PERCENT BETTER**

George Jenkins, the energetic chairman of the Publix grocery chain in Lakeland, Florida, has some unique insights into world-class management. Over the past 40 years, from most humble beginnings, Publix has become a $6 billion food-store chain that — along with Weis Markets in Pennsylvania — is one of the most profitable in the nation. The most interesting thing about Publix is that it is simply in the grocery business. Few cosmetics, magazines, books or barbecue items crowd the aisles.

Publix sells food. Many in the industry argue that food margins are simply too slim, and that the real edge comes in nonconsummable commodities. But Mr. Jenkins and his company bucked the experts and built a great organization. While much of today's business literature focuses on quantum leaps, Mr. Jenkins' philosophy is far more pragmatic. Simply, he says that each employee should attempt to do one thousand things one percent better. The cumulative impact on the bottom line would be tremendous.

MEMORANDUM

TO:

FROM:

RE: OVER, UNDER AND OUT

No one better understands the quality of management than he or she who is managed. No one has a better vantage point from which to see problems and glitches. Why, then, do evaluations in most companies flow downward, rather than upward?

MEMORANDUM

TO:

FROM:

**RE: THERE'S NOTHING WRONG
WITH SERVING A LOUSY CUP
OF COFFEE . . . OR IS THERE?**

In the tough environment of the restaurant business, more than one enterprise is looking for a unique and innovative approach to product and delivery. The great restaurateur Truett Cathy, whose Chick-fil-A chain now includes more than 600 units, has truly identified more than one key to success. But, to the amazement of his managers, Mr. Cathy proclaims that "There is nothing wrong with serving a lousy cup of coffee."

He then goes on to explain that each unit operator has the opportunity to set the tone for service and quality in his or her restaurant. Each controls what the customer sees, eats and drinks. In so doing, each has the power to establish a set of expectations. To illustrate the point, Mr. Cathy asks, "Have you ever purchased coffee from a vending machine?"

Most of us have. Was the stuff ever good? Rarely. Yet people return for more. Although that vended coffee might be all there is to choose from, customers' expectations have been managed nonetheless. Mr. Cathy suggests that there is nothing wrong with serving a lousy cup of coffee, as long as it is always lousy.

We hasten to point out that most restaurants, including Chick-fil-A, don't endorse serving bad coffee. But the notion of managing expectations does suggest an interesting insight into human nature: people often understand consistency better than they do excellence.

The management of expectations is a curious phenomenon, one that too few companies master. If you commit to high-performance service and brag about it in your advertising, you'd better deliver it every time, because customers remember. If speed is your reason for being, then perhaps you can get by with something less than prime, Colombian-grown coffee beans.

But don't make 'em wait 30 minutes for yesterday's watery brew.

MEMORANDUM

TO:

FROM:

RE: WHERE THE BUCK STARTS

If you really want to know what's wrong, you might consider talking to the experts. Who are they? They are your customers. This truth is so basic that it is often overlooked in attempts to ascertain what's wrong or right with products or services. Although the buck may stop with the person running an organization — and this is as it should be — there will be no buck if the source of the buck is neglected.

Take a look at those organizations with real staying power. You'll notice almost without exception cultures that are attuned to pleasing customers and committed to the systems and structures that further this goal.

Nestled between the Atlantic Ocean and Chesapeake Bay on Maryland's eastern shore is one of the great U.S. employers. In fact, according to Milton Moskowitz and Robert Levering, authors of The Top 100 Companies To Work For In America, Preston Corporation is one of the truly great organizations in this country. Through its six operating subsidiaries, Preston transports freight by truck. That's it. Preston Corporation is in the trucking business. However, when you listen to William Potter, Chairman of Preston, you wouldn't know if the company operates, builds or sells trucks, planes, shoes, shirts, computers or fast food. When Potter speaks about the $500 million Preston Corporation, he doesn't speak about product. He speaks primarily about customers.

Preston's commitment to excellence is so thorough-going and exemplary that it warrants repeating. This pledge to the customer is endorsed by each of the more than 8,000 employees who comprise the Preston team:

I will do everything possible to help provide my customers with superior services through innovative thinking and efficient operations. I know that our success and survival depend on how well I consistently serve our customers inside and outside the company. I understand that my job has an impact on the timeliness, quality, and cost effectiveness of what we offer. I will respect and have concern for our customers' needs. Once I make a commitment to a customer or another associate, I promise to fulfill it on time. I will do what I say, when I say I will do it. Customer satisfaction is my number one priority . . . I understand that one claim or mistake is one error too many. I promise to do my job right the first time and to continually seek performance improvement.

This statement of commitment has transformed a 66-year-old company known as "The 151 Line" (it originally started with 151 pieces of equipment) into a world-class organization. At Preston, regardless of the business, irrespective of the product line, customers are customers. Preston, like your company, is quite simply in the people business.

MEMORANDUM

TO:

FROM:

RE: RISKS AND REWARDS

Imagine this. One hundred years in business, and you now have the most recognized brand name and corporate logo in the world. Your formula for success has been a sacrosanct one that has remained unchanged for lo these many decades. A new boss arrives and asserts what is truly needed is a new product, an innovative leap, an entry to the market-place which will catapult earnings faster and farther than ever before. What is really needed is a "new Coke."

Well, that's exactly what Robert Goizueta, Chairman of the Coca-Cola Company, argued with the introduction of a new formula into the crowded and competitive soft drink market. Analysts laughed, customers screamed and employees secretly wondered.

When the shouting was over, net sales had increased almost eight percent. While the total verdict may always remain in question, Coca-Cola remained the world leader. Goizueta was unwilling to let the past rule the future and, even at this market-leading company, insisted that the greatest risk was taking no risk at all. You see, where there is no risk, there is no reward. Even market leaders must sometimes embrace change and take risks.

MEMORANDUM

TO:

FROM:

**RE: IF YOU DON'T MAKE DUST,
YOU EAT DUST**

The painting was spectacular. Perched on horseback were five vibrant young cowboys, each riding his trusty steed into a magnificent western sunset. The painting could have come out of Arizona Highways. But this four-by-six-foot oil was situated directly behind a CEO's desk. This executive had led his organization, from its start-up ten years ago, to $5 billion in annual sales — blowing away all of its competition.

A visitor was mesmerized by the painting. When the CEO left the office for a moment, the visitor dashed behind his desk to see who painted this wonderful piece. Where the artist's name should have been was a simple yet elegant inscription. As the CEO returned, he started to laugh. "Do you like that?" he asked. "I love it," the guest replied.

The CEO went on to explain that he and the company's cofounder purchased the painting the first week they were in business. It has served as a driving force behind the organization for the past decade. On the painting, under the cowhands, the inscription read, "If you don't make dust, you eat dust."

MEMORANDUM

TO:

FROM:

RE: CARPE DIEM

Not too many years ago, when it was a small, entrepreneurial firm outside Minneapolis, Minnetonka introduced the first liquid soap into a marketplace that was exclusively the domain of the bar soap business. And, not surprisingly, Minnetonka cleaned up. Competitors bigger and far older were caught napping by an aggressive neophyte far hungrier than they.

Carpe diem. Seize the day. If you snooze you lose. These are management maxims that in too many instances have been long forgotten. Business America was at one time marked by enlightened self-interest. This is, unfortunately, no longer the case. Today, hyper-aggressive competitors in many a market are not sufficiently driven by the need to seize the day, to strike while opportunity is red hot.

MEMORANDUM

TO:

FROM:

RE: THE LANGUAGE OF EXCUSES

"It sounds good, but it would never work here, because of our (A) schedule, (B) deadlines, (C) workforce, (D) payroll system, (E) manufacturing process, (F) selling season, (G) product development requirements, (H), (I), (J), (K) . . . (X), (Y) and (Z)."

That's what noted psychoanalyst/author/philosopher Thomas Szasz calls the language of excuses. The language of excuses is one of the main things that keeps companies from moving toward the 21st century. The others are fear and complacence.

Here's a suggestion for trying out new ideas.

You don't have to suddenly throw the entire organization into chaos by some radical change in the way work gets done. Take, for example, working at home. In this age of telecommunications, that will be the next great upheaval in traditional corporate structure. We suggest experimenting with a handful of people. We suggest giving the experiment at least six months to a year, because it will take that long for glitches to appear and be worked out. Give it your unqualified support. Finally, don't start it until you have brought all the potential combatants together — people who will be working at different places — and have set up ground rules.

MEMORANDUM

TO:

FROM:

RE: JOHN HENRY

"That man has done things to empower people that he doesn't even know he has done."

An employee at Atlanta's Crawford Long Hospital of Emory University said those words, in the fall of 1992, about Chief Executive Officer John Henry. The remarks were spontaneous and unsolicited.

If more American managers were able to elicit such respect and regard, none need ever lose their jobs again. They'd be too valuable to put out on the streets.

If every manager in the country were able to inspire such fealty, our productivity would soar.

MEMORANDUM

TO:

FROM:

RE: A WILL TO WIN

Take all of the truly beautiful, desirable communities in the United States. Take Palm Beach, Palm Springs, Hilton Head, the Catskills, the Rockies, Padre Island, Lake of the Ozarks and Mount Ranier. Now take Indianapolis. In his own unique, irreverent way, the great humorist Will Rodgers once described Indianapolis as "a cemetery with lights."

Well, some two decades ago, William Hudnut, an ordained minister, took Indianapolis. He was a one-term congressman who subsequently decided he could make a bigger impact on his hometown. When he was elected mayor, Bill Hudnut hit the ground running. He took a tarnished, rust-belt urban center and transformed it into a world-class city that today is regarded as the amateur sports capital of the world. Building on the foundation laid by Indiana senator Richard Lugar, Mr. Hudnut built a domed stadium. By the end of the 1980s, a multibillion-dollar infrastructure invigorated the city core, attracted world-class enterprises and enticed the Colts from Baltimore. What had been a cemetery became an economic incubator. Mr. Hudnut was driven by a sense of urgency. He had a fervor to survive and succeed. With some natural and many human resources, he rebuilt a city.

With a will to win, anything is possible.

MEMORANDUM

TO:

FROM:

**RE: SPARE THE REALITY,
AND SPOIL THE CHILD.**

Remember your college course in English poets? If you were in college long ago — when we were — you probably recall the epigrammatic poetry of Samuel Butler, a 17th-century English versemaster whose work is read today mainly in dictionaries of quotations. In fact, all you might recollect from Mr. Butler's rhymes is the line, "Spare the rod, and spoil the child."

That line has come to suggest that in order to cultivate responsible people, you have to beat up on them.

This is a distortion of Mr. Butler's intended meaning. The complete couplet says, "Love is a boy, by poets styl'd, / Then spare the rod and spoil the child."

The lesson for managers? People are intricate, precious beings who should be treated with respect. It's not that green up-and-comers — whose sense of entitlement is greater than the sum of their knowledge — should be popped into big jobs and let off the dues-paying hook. The lesson is that folks don't join a company fully formed as employees. No matter how poorly educated on the one hand, and no matter how many letters follow their names on the other, all need to do their earning by learning.

Like spinach, it's good for them. In the long run, it's good for companies.

MEMORANDUM

TO:

FROM:

**RE: PAY FOR PERFORMANCE? . . .
NEVER!**

The operant presumption in annual reviewing is that
people should have something to strive for; therefore
every employee should be found wanting, year after
year. Never tell Dick and Jane that they gave sterling
performances over the last 12 months. If you do,
they're bound to become lazy or complacent, and
competition is such that we simply cannot tolerate
complacency. Worse, they might even have the
barefaced effrontery to ask to be paid for their contributions.

This reasoning simply defies logic — and exposes the
fallacy that too often characterizes the annual review
process.

MEMORANDUM

TO:

FROM:

RE: DON'T SAY NO

The retailing industry is mired in the toughest of
times. When you combine the junk-bond mania of the
last half-decade with an uncertain economy, retail
sales are taking a nosedive. The ill-fated Campeau
Group, the bankrupt parent (facing $10 billion in
debt) of the many venerable retailers of the Allied and
Federated Groups, hit the wall as hard as any.

Through it all, though, the Rich's chain has managed
to keep its head bobbing in profitable waters . . . no
easy feat. The late Richard Rich understood the art
and science of building a billion-dollar company one
transaction and one customer at a time. Indeed, in
the toughest of times, loyalties are tenuous at best.
But the Rich's culture, honed over the past century,
continues to thrive while competitors lament the
economy.

Enter the Pink Pig. The day before Thanksgiving, the
Merlin family made its annual trek to Rich's in down-
town Atlanta to ride the famed Pink Pig. The ride,
which offered an aerial view as it encircled the
department store, had delighted children for
decades, and E. J. and Ilya were looking forward to a
treat. As the family ascended the elevator to the sixth
floor, the anticipation mounted. Onto the roof they

went to stand in what they expected to a long line packed with kids when the parents observed no line and no moving pig. On the roof was a sign proclaiming to parents that the pig looked forward to leaving her station on the day *after* Thanksgiving.

Well, the kids started to cry. Not whimper, mind you, but wail at a decibel level that brought security guards from all sides. The parents were examining their options when, fortunately, Marsha Harris appeared. Marsha works in special events at Rich's and quickly surveyed the situation. She scooped the kids up in her arms and raced over to the pig. The pig opened her doors and the kids took their traditional trip around the store. The lesson is that Marsha Harris exemplified by deed the spirit of a "don't-say-no" culture in which loyalties are built and business is won, one transaction and one customer at a time.

MEMORANDUM

TO:

FROM:

RE: MANAGEMENT BY OMISSION

Alas, nothing is forever. We knew conditions were far from robust, but now the renowned corporation is in dire straits. The Schwinn Bicycle Company has filed for Chapter 11 bankruptcy protection. Ideally, this corporation will emerge smarter and stronger. For now, seeing this happen to Schwinn is like discovering there really isn't any Santa Claus.

As kids, we hoped for Schwinns. They were the best, the aerobic equivalent of the Harley-Davidson. And while Schwinn was never truly big from a sales perspective, it was a dominant player. Eventually, it seemed to become intoxicated with its image. The company fell asleep at the wheel and got whacked by Japan and Taiwan. Perhaps what happened in recent years to Harley will be replicated at Schwinn — that is, a rebirth where demand exceeds supply and customers patiently wait in line for the pleasure of wheeling about on a Made-in-America product that has emerged as a worldwide status symbol.

Meanwhile, there are some real lessons to be learned from the Schwinn experience. None of them is new. None is unique to Schwinn. The first of them is that when you think business, you'd better think global; if commerce is not internationally focused within this tiny world of ours, it won't exist. Forget the notion that you can capture the U.S. market and not worry about the rest of the world. That would be fine if the rest of the world did not covet the U.S. market. But it does, and folks overseas are competing for dollars from consumers who will buy American only if that means buying the best. After all, people are not stupid. For their hard-earned cash they want to know they're getting quality, service and value. If it's made here, great. If not, shame on us.

Don't carp at the foreign competitor or the disloyal customer. Carp at us, the producers and businesspeople who trail the heels of reality.

Schwinn also teaches us not to manage by omission, or looking the other way. Consider things always broken. There is always a better way simply because the world is constantly changing. We can't make the point too strongly: change is the status quo.

MEMORANDUM

TO:

FROM:

**RE: GO AHEAD, LET ME HAVE IT . . .
I CAN TAKE IT**

Frank Perdue, Chairman of Perdue Farms, one of the largest integrated poultry operations in the world, is a distinct kind of guy. Mr. Perdue is perhaps one of the very few CEOs in America who looks like his products. Think about it. Donald Petersen (Ford Motor Co.) did not have the look of a Mustang. Allen Jacobson (3M) does not resemble Scotch tape. And Irvine Hockaday, Jr., simply doesn't come across like a Hallmark Card. Mr. Perdue, on the other hand, comes at you like a solid, healthy Rhode Island Red. In building this $2 billion organization, he has been obsessed with product quality and service delivery. Both inside and outside the organization, he has challenged all to tell him what they like and dislike.

Mr. Perdue, you see, understands that the heart and soul of any world-class organization is the ability to learn from its successes and take from its mistakes. Continuous improvement is the order of the day, and the only way to ensure that is to ask for it. What distinguishes Perdue products in a crowded, competitive marketplace is its leader's willingness to do whatever it is that must be done and to hear what needs to be said. This is great management at work.

MEMORANDUM

TO:

FROM:

**RE: MONEY IS STILL A SOCIALLY
ACCEPTABLE WAY OF SAYING
I LOVE YOU**

We could say "talk is cheap," but it's been said before.
You can't talk "private enterprise and initiative" while
stubbornly compensating folks on a mass, across-
the-board basis. If you want high performance, there
should be a direct relationship between what people
do and what they receive, between productivity and
pay. If you want extraordinary performance, compensation should not be viewed as a maintenance factor,
but rather as a vehicle for letting people know that
there is a linear relationship between what they
invest in their work and how they are rewarded.

The American Dream is relatively simple to understand. In essence, it focuses on behavior, not birth. It
says that education plus dedication (a little luck
won't hurt, either) can make the dream a functioning
reality. Outstanding organizations endorse the
dream, pay the price, and breed winners. The others
endorse the dream, don't ante up, and run the good
people away.

Pep talks don't pay bills. Each of us usually wants to
know we're not getting lost in the shuffle.

MEMORANDUM

TO:

FROM:

RE: REMEMBER THE FRONT LINE

It was 10:30 on a Saturday night. Nothing too special about this particular weekend evening. The baby was sleeping . . . maybe. The latest video release was playing on the VCR and the third bowl of popcorn was almost empty. Then it happened. The telephone rang. Late Saturday night — who in the world would be calling?

"Hello," she said. "This is Tammy Senkbeil, calling from Giant Foods. We owe you some money." Sure enough, the family had been grocery shopping earlier that day and had, indeed, cashed a check at the Giant Foods store. Tammy (a cashier at Giant) was closing out her register that evening when she noticed a discrepancy, and after 45 minutes of auditing her checks, she found the problem and called the family with the news. Giant owed the couple nine dollars. Certainly no monumental sum, but a monumental concern for Tammy at 10:30 on a Saturday evening. Interestingly, the couple did not have an address or telephone number printed on the check. But Tammy persevered, tracked the couple down, and in the middle of a very mediocre Western and at the end of her very long day, simply took the time and the effort to call.

Hail to the champion . . . who takes the little bit of

effort to make loyal customers fiercely loyal. Hail to the front line. Hail to a company that reflects excellence at every operating level. Chairman Israel Cohen of multibillion-dollar, Washington, D.C.-based Giant Foods has built a first-class organization on first-class, front-line representatives. Cohen has built a company of champions at every rung of the corporate ladder where seller meets buyer. Giant foods has become a giant in its industry because of the attention to detail at each and every level of the firm. Even in the largest organizations, transactions descend to simple contacts between buyers and sellers. In corporate giants, the team members on the front line, at the sales counter, the register, and the teller window can — and do — make the difference between the champion and the has-been. Cohen's commitment, fortified by Tammy's delivery, assures each and every current and prospective customer of first-class treatment each and every time.

This is the stuff of which good businesses are made.

MEMORANDUM

TO:

FROM:

RE: THE TROUBLE WITH FEAR

W. Edwards Deming is a 93-year-old, Wyoming-bred statistician whose half-century of work on an elusive ideal called "quality" didn't make a dent in America's wayward, management-by-objective mindset until 1980. That year, a television program titled "If Japan Can, Why Can't We" hurled the Deming name into the spotlight. Since then, notions about monitoring productivity and improving quality have bred all the faddishness and opportunism that are inevitably born with each new theoretical litter. But Deming's ideas have also sparked serious discussion about the conditions under which U.S. capitalism expects people to function. Among the more entrenched of those is the fear-based environment.

The most debilitating aspect of the work force is not low pay or dangerous conditions. It's fear, and it has been around since the first person exchanged independence and autonomy for work and wages.

Fear drives the actions of the competent as predictably as it governs the excuses of the incompetent.

Otherwise promising managers are afraid to challenge the way the boss has always done things. Subordinates jockeying for position learn to mime, not to invent. Because of fear, all are taught to guard their flanks, whatever the cost to others, to themselves or to the company.

The trouble with fear is that it snuffs out self-regard. Fearful people perform because they're afraid not to. Sturdy people perform because they'd be embarrassed not to.

MEMORANDUM

TO:

FROM:

RE: THE BEST MANAGERS

Although Atilla the Hun might have struck some as a good manager, he wouldn't — and shouldn't — last long in today's empowered workplace. But neither should managers who might be named Pollyanna, Iago or Dr. Faustus. As far as we can tell, the best managers are those who:

- Learn from their mistakes and spend more time growing from the experience than bewailing it.
- Act like sponges, absorbing all the wisdom available to them, then making the most honest decisions they can make.
- Are forgiving, but not foolish.
- Strive to be compassionate without being gutless.

MEMORANDUM

TO:

FROM:

RE: CORPORATE RX:
     NO FOUNTAIN OF YOUTH

In the world of business, nothing is forever. Corporate longevity is fragile and ephemeral. Organizational health and prosperity involve continuous renewal rather than a futile search for some kind of fountain of youth. After all, this wellspring eluded Ponce de Leon — and he was an experienced explorer.

How can organizations stay healthy, recognizing they're not likely to live forever? Essentially, it is a case of doing the right things, including the following:

  1. Anticipate and embrace change. Being adaptive or reactive simply won't get the job done.
  2. Always search for a better way. If you don't, some present or future competitor will. Playing catch-up in business is no fun.
  3. While never neglecting the immediate, develop a long-term perspective that addresses the interests of all stakeholders and constituencies.
  4. Build on basics.

The true secret is that there is no secret.

MEMORANDUM

TO:

FROM:

RE: GOOD FOLKS ARE HARD TO FIND

Good people are hard to find. How's that for a bit of wisdom? Folks have been looking for other good folks as long as there have been folks, and the search continues. In all likelihood, it always will. So let's recognize that in all too many instances, it's not so much a matter what people a business gets, but what it does with them after they arrive. Look to the present and the future and mold the best from what you get. After all, this is what managers are paid to do and this is what real leadership is all about. Furthermore, it's the only game in town.

He certainly looked like a winner. An honor student, he had worked his way through college in a co-op program and had finished in record time. He was smart, hungry, and ambitious. He also wanted out after eight months on the job. Let's try to understand why.

Be assured, it was not money. It was challenge and an opportunity to utilize his skills and energy. When he communicated these feelings and frustrations to his boss, he was promised more money and a transfer to another location where he would "cool it" for a couple of years until the company could properly use what he had to offer. Apparently, the idea of being placed in cold storage (CS) for two years was not too appealing. Then he really wanted out.

Somewhere, there is a message. Can any organization be so blessed that it can afford to CS talented staff members? Expressed another way, can any organization maintain its effectiveness and profitability by CS-ing its talent? When this route is taken, what impact does it have on the people in CS, and what does it do to the organization? You do not have to be a management expert or a student of organization to know the correct answer. Therefore, the crucial issues are, why are these practices in use, and what practices should take their place?

MEMORANDUM

TO:

FROM:

RE: ODE TO ACTIVITY

Beware of activity for its own sake. Think for a moment about some of the institutionalized practices in your company, things that might have been based on reality 25 years ago, but which seem silly now. The only reason to cling to them is that they represent the way things have always been done. We bet they include "face time."

This is the attitude that everyone must work in the office all the time: "The only good employee is the visible employee and, if I can't see you, then you are not working." In an age of telecommunications, this is patently absurd. Its only lingering contribution to the organization is the comfort it offers those managers who believe that they need bodies to supervise.

Winning organizations will measure achievement, not activity. For example, meetings are held to enhance effectiveness, and people are brought together to help themselves and the organization. Meetings are not held just to have something to do and keep folks out of mischief. In winning organizations, achievement, not hours, is the measure. Burning the midnight oil is commendable if meaningful things occur. It is dysfunctional if it becomes a hollow ritual reinforced by a corporate culture that equates achievement with time spent. Such a culture leads to form, not function — and it will cause winners to look for greener pastures, also-rans to adapt, and the unproductive to think they are in heaven.

MEMORANDUM

TO:

FROM:

**RE: TRUE PARTICIPATION
    DEMANDS ACCOUNTABILITY**

True participation means not only that I don't have to brook your tyranny, but also that I do have to take a complete measure of responsibility for my contributions or lack thereof.

True participation does not signify the survival of the fittest carnivore. Neither should it imply survival of the most accomplished sycophant.

True participation creates an environment in which it is possible for people to wish each other well. Its shuns scapegoating. It places a premium on delivering and on accountability.

True participation anticipates the best from everyone. As a continuous process, its aim is to foster a culture as unique and free as the tyrannical culture was stereotypical and shackled. If you see it in action, it will take your breath away.

In organizations where people feel good about themselves, they also tend to feel good about others:

"It's a great day at the Radisson," she said. Actually, it was 20 degrees and snowing in Rochester, but the receptionist, the front-line representative of this first-class, multibillion-dollar hotelier, was communicating an honest-to-goodness, feel-good attitude that's neutralizing at worst and doggone catchy at best (even to crabby parties on the other end of a 5:30 a.m. wake-up call!). In this type of culture, people start pulling and cheering for one another. A far cry from the usual — where people wish you well, but not too well.

At a Kimberly-Clark plant, shift-change information meetings are hotbeds of production discussion. There, teams of colleagues have gleefully discarded the "it's-not-my-job" mindset and replaced it with team-developed goals, plans and rewards. Employees feel consensus builds commitment and commitment reinforced with rewards builds profits.

The champion manager wants to make certain that work, in the words of the late Abraham Maslow, becomes a self-actualizing experience that is "as normal and natural as eating or breathing." In world-class organizations, people know their work is important. They understand how their individual jobs fit into the whole. They comprehend what their company is all about, and this shared vision is a requisite for developing an organizational personality, where, when people come to work each day, what they do, morally and ethically, is whatever it is that has to be done.

MEMORANDUM

TO:

FROM:

RE: IMPROVING THE RIGHT
    EQUIPMENT

Productive behavior merits praise and thanks. The winning manager wins because his or her staff exhibits winning behavior, and this pattern eventually becomes a way of life. Creating a winning climate is simply one dimension. Maintaining, expanding, and strengthening this climate is another.

Doing both often consists of paying careful attention to the so-called little things. In a recent poll administered by the U.S. Chamber of Commerce and the Gallup Organization, the following question was asked: "What do you think it would be possible to change so as to bring about the largest improvement in performance and productivity in most companies?" Over 80 percent of those responding cited worker attitudes and abilities, and managerial attitudes and abilities. Only a very small percentage thought that enhanced computer facilities or more modernized plants and equipment would make a significant difference.

Attitudes? Abilities? At the same time we are proclaiming loudly to the world at large that intensive capital reinvestment and the inundation of the corporate arena with super-computers is our only hope for economic salvation, the greatest perceived drag on performance and productivity, the albatross around the collective necks of corporate America, appears to be the millions of employees who are not challenged, charged, and rewarded.

In a similar nationwide survey conducted by A.B. Dick Company in Chicago, the results indicated that "lack of recognition and equipment breakdown were Americans' most frustrating on-the-job experiences." It is relatively easy to fix equipment, but the radical surgery needed to reshape and repair employee and managerial attitudes is complex, costly and critical.

MEMORANDUM

TO:

FROM:

RE: TALES TOLD BY A FEARMONGER

Yarns about fear are as tenacious as they are destructive. One is that fear makes people productive.

It does not. Fear may make people "work" harder, or appear to do so, but it holds captive the most critical elements of productivity, which are enthusiasm, candor and resourcefulness.

Another fearmonger's tale is that fear spurs competition, which is good because competitors are achievers.

Wrong again. Corporate competition in America is orchestrated to set people against each other for rewards that have little to do with maturity. It rewards ends and forgets about means. Fear among supervisory personnel leads to connivance and reluctance to credit others. Among non-supervisory personnel, fear spawns silence and leads to defensiveness, rigidity and smallness — i.e., to doing only what you're paid to do.

Fear is expressed through bitterness. Why in the world would companies want corps of bitter people? Bitter people do little, either for themselves or for their employers, that is worthwhile over the long haul.

MEMORANDUM

TO:

FROM:

RE: MANAGEMENT BY TIMIDITY

If you, the manager, won't stand up to the resident bully, won't correct the office whiner, or won't confront the chronic underminer, how can you expect your staff to stand up for you?

MEMORANDUM

TO:

FROM:

RE: CORNY IS GOOD

We all know the mail-order catalog business is a competitive marketplace and that the players change regularly. The successful firms know that the magic of home shopping is convenience, timeliness, and responsiveness to an increasingly demanding consumer audience.

One of the greats in the industry is The Right Start. Stan, Lenny, and The Right Start Family, headquartered in Westlake Village, California, have a customer pledge that is clearly understood and accepted by each member of the Right Start team. You see, The Right Start sells high-quality products for infants and young children. The company's philosophy has catapulted this firm to a preeminent position in its marketing segment. Its customer commitment says it all:

Satisfaction Guaranteed Absolutely. If you are for any reason dissatisfied with any item received from The Right Start Catalog, please return the item for a prompt refund or, if you prefer, exchange. Your baby deserves the best.

The creed may be old-fashioned, corny, and folksy, but it certainly is profitable. The great revelation is that when old-fashioned and corny and folksy are fortified with delivery, customers respond. The Right Start has bridged the gulf between what they say and do, and the marketplace has enthusiastically responded.

MEMORANDUM

TO:

FROM:

RE: KEEP YOUR EYE ON THE BALL: MANAGING INDIVIDUAL DIFFERENCES

In the literal sense, an organization is a goal-attaining conveyance where people accomplish collectively what they cannot do individually. It is a conscious banding and bonding process and, finally, a way for getting from where you are to where you want to be. Where you want to be is the destination point, the bull's-eye, the target. Again, we are focusing on where the organization can take us rather than on the mere process of organizing.

Now, what does all of this mean in regard to diversity, gender, ethnicity and other matters of individual difference and/or preference? It means, if managers keep an eye on the ball, their primary focus is on behavior, not birth. Not only is this focus consistent with sound administration, but it is fully in harmony with an essential tenet of the private enterprise system: an individual's position in the organization should be inextricably bound to her or his contribution, and, therefore, there should be a high degree of correlation between this contribution and compensation. Admittedly, this is the ideal, but it is one that should be strived for if we are to be both competitive and successful in a global society where results will ultimately make the difference.

Properly managed, the organization can transform a collection of diverse individuals into a powerful goal-attaining mechanism. Focusing on function, not form; on deliverables, not differences or similarities; on performance, not prejudice — this appears to be sound in both theory and practice. This is what enlightened management is all about.

MEMORANDUM

TO:

FROM:

**RE: THE GET-IT-RIGHT-
THE-FIRST-TIME MENTALITY**

Why not consciously strive for flawless service and perfect products the very first time around? Decide that errors and flaws are unacceptable. This does not mean perfection will be attained. It does mean that near-misses are simply not acceptable. The right-the-first-time mentality is a characteristic of great organizations that recognize there is always a better way. In organizations of this nature, a premium is placed on individual performance through a system that truly recognizes and rewards the good things emanating from first-time results.

Perfection. When was the last time you observed, experienced, or participated in perfection? When was the last time you witnessed a flawless performance, purchased a flawless product, or were treated with flawless service? Can you recollect receiving excellent treatment or accurate delivery in the past week, month or year?

Perfection, flawlessness, excellence, and accuracy are words that seldom come to mind these days. Indeed, terms like these are difficult for many of us to vocalize. We have for all too long accepted the mundane, promoted the average and rewarded the mediocre.

But in today's global business community populated by aggressive, hungry, ambitious competitors, nothing short of perfection will do. We must put to rest the notion that excellence represents fantasy, not fact, in organizational life today. The gauntlet has been cast; the challenge has been made. In the game of winners and losers, losing is no fun. And in business there is just no such thing as a good loser.

Nothing but perfection is acceptable. Nothing but perfection should be rewarded.

Motorola, the worldwide electronics company, has 90,000 employees deeply committed to the pursuit of perfection. Motorola's Participative Management Program (PMP) is a system that allows labor and management to collectively pursue excellence at work. At Motorola semiconductor plants in Mesa, Arizona, and Austin, Texas, PMP participants have established awards that are granted for achieving but a single standard: 100 percent, unequivocal perfection. To date, 3,648 Perfection Awards have been won at the Mesa facility. A Perfection Award was recently won by 20 production employees in Austin who delivered 2.1 million units without a single defect. The success of PMP and the Perfection Awards are a result of an effective top-to-bottom commitment to perfection that is encouraged and reinforced throughout Motorola.

It is the little things that count. But too often, it is the little things that we simply forget.

MEMORANDUM

TO:

FROM:

RE: KEEP THAT MORAL OUTRAGE

"Why don't you grow up?" the industry guru sneers grandly at the callow manager. "Haven't you learned by now that people just do things like that?"

The setting is an impromptu conference. The subject at hand, how one industry is doing and where it is headed, has in the course of conversation expanded to include lying, questionable deal-making and me-first amorality among certain executives. The guru, who's been around long enough to get a good look at the underbelly of human nature, is of the opinion that people just do things that are no damn good, and the fact that they happen somehow renders them acceptable. Furthermore, he reckons, anyone who expects people to be otherwise — to exercise some kind of principled self-restraint — is a simpleton deserving not respect, but scorn.

The guru is hopelessly jaded. And he is totally wrong. The best thing that can happen in today's companies is that they be led by people who have not, could not, and will never lose their sense of moral outrage. It's the only thing that stays the hand of barbarism.

MEMORANDUM

TO:

FROM:

**RE: IF YOU DRIVE OUT FEAR,
MUST YOU USHER IN CHAOS?**

Absolutely not. Getting shed of management by intimidation does not imply intimidation of management. Allowing freedom to speak one's mind is not the same as courting anarchy.

You don't want a population of hotheads, because they rarely think straight. But neither do you want organizations full of toadies, because they rarely think at all.

Driving out fear does not mean excusing people from responsibility. It does not mark the abolition of respect and good manners.

Instead, it suggests an attitude such as this: "When I am afraid of you, I fear you will hurt me. When I respect you, I assume you will help me."

MEMORANDUM

TO:

FROM:

**RE: LET'S GET REAL ABOUT
    EVALUATIONS**

Why do employers collect yearly evaluations of their employees and tuck them away in personnel files? The reasons given are, variously, that:

- Evaluations allow people to know how they are regarded by their supervisors.
- Evaluations are useful because as they articulate employees' strengths and weaknesses; they provide the motivation to improve.
- Evaluations assure people that everyone is treated fairly — measured, as it were, by the same stick.

The real reason, more often than not, has little to do with any of that. The real reason is fear of lawsuits. Rather than honestly acknowledging the true game and establishing rules that everyone understands, companies start contests. These inevitably become paranoid jousts of who can best second-guess whom. They play out something like this:

- We recognize that Jane or Dick belongs to a category protected by the Equal Employment Opportunity Commission. However inept Jane and Dick may be, we know we can't fire them without risking trouble, so we prepare before the fact.

- We've tried Jane in this job and have found her wanting.

Although she might do well in another job, we're afraid she won't be mature enough to handle the move. So, rather than putting her and us out of our collective misery, we extend it. But while we're doing that, we collect evidence that Jane, not her manager, has been the incompetent party.

- Dick has the personality of a cobra, the tact of a fishwife and the manners of a spoiled brat. But he is smart and quickly masters the mechanics of any job assigned to him. In the evaluation, does Dick's supervisor confront his real problem in the workplace, which is the attitude and self-centeredness that have become legendary in the department? No. The supervisor covers ground the firm's lawyers have recommended. Both Dick and his supervisor keep their jobs while losing the point.

What's the flawed reasoning here? It is that having it down on paper that Dick or Jane was repeatedly warned about his or her functioning — or evaluated on irrelevant terms — isn't ever going to prevent a lawsuit. It will merely give the company a better defense. Whatever the outcome, costs will be incurred.

MEMORANDUM

TO:

FROM:

RE: LISTENING AND RESPONDING

Picture this: a birthing room at a first-class hospital equipped with the latest in medical equipment. The parents had devoted two months to a comprehensive review of Lamaze techniques and were following their training vigorously. The doctor was doing her job quietly and professionally. The mother was in constant communication with one of the two delivery-room nurses, who was supportive, attentive and compassionate — not undesirable traits for a line representative of any organization.

As the moment approached, the anxious mother-to-be, seeking simply to be kept informed regarding the position of the baby, exclaimed, "Please, tell me what's happening." A second delivery-room nurse, who had the bedside manner of Attila the Hun and the empathy of a water buffalo, stepped up to the bed and responded in a saccharine tone, "Dear . . . you're having a baby!" You can imagine the mother's — a.k.a. customer's — reaction. She lurched off the bed and threatened to strangle the offending nurse. Fortunately, the baby was born soon after, even though the doctor believes to this day that the customer's rage probably accelerated the blessed event.

The nurse's attitude reflects a problem common to

many service-related businesses. The line person delivering service to a stressed-out, overly concerned, hyper-demanding customer assumes the customer simply wouldn't understand the technical aspects of the delivery. Good or bad, right or wrong, this front-line representative believed the customer was ignorant and incapable of understanding the biomedical phenomenon of birth, though fully capable of understanding the act of paying the hospital for its services.

The assumption that the marketplace doesn't know and doesn't care is a dangerous one. The management of enterprises must recognize that today's customer is better educated, informed, and able to differentiate right from wrong than ever before in the history of business as we know it. The consuming public reads, observes and chooses in a more knowledgeable manner than most companies would admit. The nurse's assumption that the customer couldn't possibly understand the intricacies of the moment is repeated daily in millions of transactions between buyers and sellers. Time invested in explaining, detailing and responding represents an investment on the part of vendors and reveals commitment to prospective buyers. Given that, in the long run, companies can and will develop and refine quality products and quality services, the value added will occur at the level where transactions are conducted, where sellers meet buyers.

MEMORANDUM

TO:

FROM:

RE: HONESTY IS THE BEST POLICY . . . REALLY

Talk about business under fire . . . the brokerage industry seems to fuel the flames. The securities industry is a rough-and-tumble business, not for the weak of heart or spirit. At Legg Mason, the Baltimore-based holding company engaged in securities brokerage, trading, underwriting and investment management, chairman Chip Mason has built one of the ten largest firms in the country on an ethos of honesty.

In a recent address, Mason listed honesty as the number one business principle at Legg Mason, followed by: 2) customers must make great deals of money, and 3) don't be greedy. Since 1983, Legg Mason has annually increased its number of brokers by about 20 percent, and among 25 securities brokers (traded on all three major markets), it has seen revenue growth in the past five years that trails only Morgan Stanley. The winning attitude at Legg Mason permeates the entire organization because of Chip Mason's obsession. Mason's personal code has become the professional code for the entire organization — and customers and the company benefit from it.

Mark Twain once wrote: "To be good is noble. To tell

people how to be good is even nobler, and much less trouble." The difference at Legg Mason is Chip Mason's realization that you don't change others without setting the example yourself.

MEMORANDUM

TO:

FROM:

**RE: ISN'T THE SAME OLD,
SAME OLD TOO OLD?**

In any endeavor, the key elements are goals, people and structure. Perhaps because it is difficult to understand, structure — or the design of the enterprise — is often treated like an orphan. It should not be, for structure is the thing that enables organizations to move from one place to another, much as planes and automobiles move people. Unfortunately, while those modes of transportation have changed, organizational design has stayed much the same since Old Testament times. Its pyramidal shape could have been fashioned by Jethro, father-in-law of Moses and arguably the world's first management consultant.

In advising Moses to appoint rulers over thousands, hundreds, fifties and tens, didn't Jethro create the first hierarchical organization? Surely so, and it seemed to work for him. We don't think it works nearly so well now, especially in modern banking.

Throughout the 1970s, banks earned about 80 cents a year for each $100 of loans and booked investment securities. Today, comparable earnings have dropped below 50 cents per $100. At the start of the 1980s, banks' personnel expenses were 1.8 times profits. By

1990, they were profits multiplied by 3.3. The worst-managed and designed banks spend 30 to 40 percent more delivering the same products and services as the best-led and most efficiently structured financial institutions.

What might Jethro say, were he alive today? That we have beaten a good thing to death. If we don't want more of the same, we must confront organizational structure head on, and change it. The skin-deep approach — tinkering with goals and folks — is dated and ineffectual. Whether we're committed enough to redesign the structure of enterprise is another matter. Some companies, like Wachovia Bank, have been committed since the beginning. Indeed, the "personal banking" design is the embodiment of delegation, empowerment and responsible decision-making. For it, Wachovia wins the gold.

Without something similar, many other companies will come away with nothing. In them, the structure is shattered. Patch-jobs, mindless downsizing and other superficial remedies won't do the trick.

MEMORANDUM

TO:

FROM:

**RE: THINK BUSINESS AND
    THINK INTERNATIONAL**

Forget what many of the experts say. There is no such thing as international business. The designation "international" has become an anachronism. It is a dinosaur.

Remember this if you are on the producing or receiving end. Whether you are manufacturing goods or providing services, you are competing with others who are courting your customers. These others are likely to come from places whose names we can't even pronounce — much to our shame. On the other hand, if you are a consumer spending hard-earned bucks, you are looking for the best. Many times this means it will not carry a made-in-the-good-old-USA label.

If we're serious about turning things around, we need to objectively determine how we got the way we are. Next, we must make absolutely certain we commit ourselves to being the best — the best anywhere. Anywhere, you understand, is anywhere in the world. After all, your customers bring the world into their homes several hours a day by simply turning on television sets. P. T. Barnum may have been correct about a sucker being born every minute, but today, fewer and fewer customers remain naive about the marketplace. Hence, think business and think international. If you're not doing this, you may not be thinking at all.

MEMORANDUM

TO:

FROM:

RE: ON RESPECT

Understand that some people will never respect you. Either they're incapable of respecting any authority figure, or they're too anal retentitive to give any manager his or her due.

MEMORANDUM

TO:

FROM:

RE: QUALITY IN TWO SIMPLE STEPS

Amidst all the hoopla about quality, zero-defect performance and the bottom line, there are still two simple steps that must be followed if an organization, public or private, large or small, is to remain competitive. They are:

1. Do it right. Everyone's job should be done right the first time.
2. Do the right thing —for your customer and for your company.

The fact is, quality service provided by quality people really does make the difference. Location, product, and a host of other variables can generate a competitive edge in the short-run. The winners always strive to deliver the best in the best possible way. Two examples:

The automobile, an expensive one, was brand new but had to be towed back to the shop four times in less than one month. It had probably traveled more miles backwards than forwards. While the customer was unhappy and disappointed, he noticed that in each instance the dealer's staff responded with a sense of immediacy and concern. They appeared to be as upset with the situation as the customer was.

On the fourth occasion, the dealer, Robert Hennessy, told the customer that his service department would eventually determine the cause of the breakdowns, but the customer had already been inconvenienced far too much. Therefore, Hennessy suggested the customer select another brand-new automobile from his inventory. The customer did, the replacement was trouble-free, and Hennessy and his personnel added a pleased patron to their sales force at no additional cost. While this incident occurred several years ago, the customer has never forgotten, and the experience has been a plus for both the dealer and the customer.

The Sengos in California sell delicious dried fruit. So do a lot of other folks. However, they seem to do it with a special sense of dedication and purpose. They appear to have a real handle on the quality formula. Recently, a pleased, not merely satisfied, customer received this note with his order: "Enclosed is a $1.00 refund for overpayment. Our new prices are lower. Thank you, the Sengos."

As far as our customer is concerned, the Sengos now have a monopoly on shipping dried fruit to him — and whomever else he can contact.

Again, quality = products + people. This formula assures that everyone can get well together. After all, whether it's transportation or food, a couple of bucks or several thousands of dollars, isn't this what excellence is all about?

MEMORANDUM

TO:

FROM:

RE: MANAGEMENT BY COMMISSION

Hey there, boss. Where were you when the manners were handed out? You'd be a fool to treat your superiors, your customers or your suppliers the way you've treated me this past year, because they could retaliate against you and enhance your reputation as a real creep. Why do you persist in making a fool of yourself — and a wreck of your subordinate — when you relate to me?

Why is it so difficult for you to show to me a respect similar to that you display to other people whose good will is essential to your success? I'd be very grateful if you'd quit doing the following:

- Calling me at home for no good reason.
- Telling me something is voluntary and then forcing me to do it.
- Lambasting me in front of other people.
- Expecting me to tell you things that are none of your business.
- Asking me to lie for you.
- Never giving me credit for my ideas because you're busily using them to impress your superiors.
- Crying wolf when there is no wolf around.

MEMORANDUM

TO:

FROM:

RE: READY, AIM, BLAME

If the company fails to win the big contract, if the product doesn't sell, if the crowds don't come, if the deadline is not met, it is not the end of the world and should not be treated as such.

Nothing that happens in an ordinary company remotely approaches the import of war, hunger, the suffering of the poor or the mistreatment of living creatures.

When a mistake is made or money lost, it's important to consider these things before taking aim at the people who screwed up. (The responsible party may have been the system). Rages, hysterics and blame will not help a bad situation.

MEMORANDUM

TO:

FROM:

RE: PEOPLE WHO WILL
    LET YOU HAVE IT

One of the most beloved corporate buzzwords of our time is "feedback." Its definition is "the fact of, or the enthusiasm for, candid opinions about how one is doing as a company, a manager or a rank-and-file employee."

Petitioning for feedback is regarded as a particularly vital exercise for up-and-coming executives. Not only does it assure knowledge of intricate functional and sociological happenings in their sundry departments, but also it identifies those budding managers as people who are patient enough to listen, strong enough to hear and mature enough to judge the value of what is said to them.

If you've recently been promoted to that first manager's job, here — for your education or amusement — is a partial list of the kinds of people who may offer you feedback. The hardest task you will ever have will be separating the wheat from the chaff, the reasonable from the self-serving, the potential allies from the irredeemable blackguards.

- Attila and Attilette. These lovely people want to intimidate you. Whether they engage you in combat during staff meetings or overpower you with their authoritative rhetoric, the first item on their agenda is to make you feel that there's no hope for you as a manager.

■ Uriah and Urianna. Ever hear of Uriah Heep, the groveling, ingratiating and treacherous bookkeeper in Charles Dickens' novel *David Copperfield*? He could take lessons from these two namesakes. They'll cling to you like leeches, savoring your every confidence — and logging your every mistake. They don't necessarily want your job — though either would sigh dolefully and accept it if offered. What they want is to derive benefit from your status in the company. Just be aware that your sterling character and managerial gifts aren't the reason these folks seem to be so fond of you.

■ Elmira and Elmer. Alas, they are scared witless of you, not because you are some kind of banshee, but because they are frightened of authority figures. Whether their apprehensions present themselves through whispering to themselves, in bullying others or by marked buck-passing, Elmer and Elmira can't think for themselves. Beware.

■ Rowan and Rowena. If ever anyone took pleasure in trying to sabotage fellow employees, it's these two snipers. They neither care nor bother to find out whether or not their colleagues represent potential competitors. That doesn't matter to them. What does matter is not taking the chance. So everyone is first subject to their perusal, and then to their criticisms. All offered to you in a spirit of helpfulness, of course, and for the sake of the company.

MEMORANDUM

TO:

FROM:

RE: MANAGE FOR MORE

How often do we hear, "I'll get by" or "It's good enough" or "They will never know the difference" or "It's not my job"? Too often. In today's hypercompetitive marketplace, getting by doesn't cut it anymore. Managing the human factor, managing for more, and providing lagniappe — the little extra that no one expected — will create such a memorable impression that most customers will come back for more, whether they need it or not. Conversely, alienating the consuming public by refusing to take a bit of initiative will come back to haunt any organization.

A great wedding was planned at a grand old hotel in Chattanooga. Family members and friends had booked more than 100 rooms for the entire weekend's festivities. Dinners, receptions and other revenue-generating events were all planned. Guest number 101 called from Phoenix to reserve a suite and a crib, but encountered a problem — no more cribs. According to the reservationist, not a single crib remained in the entire hotel for that festive weekend. Now instead of suggesting, "We'll find you one — even if we have to rent it elsewhere," the clerk cloddishly suggested that perhaps the couple could bring their own crib, or better yet, leave the baby at home. Rather than seizing the moment and emerging a hero, the clerk raised a customer's anxiety to new, unforeseen levels.

Managing for more places the onus on all. Providing value-added service is a top-to-bottom phenomenon that must be continuously reinforced and refined. This situation was an easy one to solve — that's the good news. The bad news is that most problems are easy ones that are mismanaged, mishandled, misdirected and messed up. Whether it was a crib, refrigerator, blanket, VCR or unedited version of *Gone With The Wind* makes no difference. Managing for more means simply doing whatever one has to do to get the job done.

MEMORANDUM

TO:

FROM:

RE: SHOOTING YOURSELF IN THE FOOT: AN ART AND A SCIENCE

"Forget the customer. He or she can wait. We've got bigger fish to fry. Let's get manufacturing".

If you think this is one company psyching itself up for a battle with a competitor, think again. It's one segment of an organization gearing itself up for a blood-bath with one of its own parts. Kind of a corporate auto-cannibalism. Unusual? Not one bit. Dysfunctional? Absolutely. Industrial sociologists have labeled this self-destructive process "segmentation," or a situation in which one part of an organization attempts to build its prestige and status on the ruins of another. This is internecine warfare of the corporate type and, like all struggles of this nature, it results in everyone getting hurt. No one prospers.

No one, that is, except the company's competitors, who are able to capitalize on the inability of the firm to pull together and stay focused on those factors that actually contribute to the well-being of all stakeholders.

Take a look at your own organization. Is teamwork or scapegoating the mode? If the response is scape-goating, all of the jobs are in jeopardy, customers will suffer and alert competitors will assuredly fill all those vacuums that segmentation creates.

MEMORANDUM

TO:

FROM:

RE: CONSTRUCTIVE CHAOS

In the cliché hall of fame, the adage "if it ain't broke, don't fix it" ranks right near the top. However, it sounds far better than it works. As a matter of plain, simple fact, in business it rarely works at all. A sounder maxim might be "there is always a better way, and being the best is not the permanent possession of anyone."

Perfection in business is not an absolute state or final destination. Rather, it is like a moving target. Therefore, delivering the best in product or service requires a type of corporate restlessness where the collective eye is always on the ball, and the ball is always the customer, and the customer is always like a member of the family.

MEMORANDUM

TO:

FROM:

RE: MAKE CUSTOMERS EXPERTS

Let's look at cookies. In the world of baking, cookies are commodities. Sure, some are soft, others hard. Some are thick, many thin, but when all is said and done, the cookie product is a basic commodity that many work hard at differentiating from the thousands of competitive products on the market.

Few people focus on cookie basics better than Michael Coles, chairman of The Great American Cookie Company. In good times and not so good times, Coles' cookie business has boomed. In Michael's own words, "The industry has made experts out of our customers." Today, 13 years after its founding and with more than 400 stores coast to coast and in Guam, The Great American Cookie Company reconfirms weekly the basics that have distinguished this firm from everyone else in the business.

Every Wednesday, a cross-section of team members meets to introduce new products, recipes and ideas. It took three years to perfect a chocolate cheesecake product, but this same attention to detail enables some units to gross in excess of $30,000 on certain days . . . and that's a lot of cookies. The punchline here is that there are virtually no single-unit franchise owners, but rather a team full of owners who started with one and have continued, year in and year out, to invest in the same basics that have made this firm the industry leader. It's simple, it's controllable, it's commodities, it's cookies. The basics hold true for all of us.

MEMORANDUM

TO:

FROM:

RE: REWARDING STUPIDITY

Accountability is not achieved when you pamper people's weaknesses under the guise of running a "compassionate workplace." Accountability occurs when you help people grow strong within an atmosphere of clear, fair and consistent expectations. If some managers can't evoke that, or if some people can't rise to it, then neither are suited to the jobs they hold.

As consultant Morris Shechtman is fond of saying, "Empowering people is not the same as rewarding stupidity."

MEMORANDUM

TO:

FROM:

RE: DO THE RIGHT THING

There's no such thing as business ethics. Now, before the antiestablishment chorus wails, "We told you so," let us explain. Ethics are ethics whether we're talking about business, government, labor, education, the arts and sciences or whatever. As the more hip among our readers might observe, that is precisely what moviemaker Spike Lee opined in *Do the Right Thing*. While we agree with Mr. Lee, he didn't coin the phrase or invent the notion. In fact, this type of sage advice has been around from the beginning, and we're not going to debate just when that was. Perhaps it came from Leviticus. There, in the third book of the Old Testament, "Do not pervert justice" referred to length, weight and quantity. It meant using honest measures. Today, the phrase means doing the right thing. It means making sure that everything you do — as a company or as an individual within it — can stand being seen in the light of day.

MEMORANDUM

TO:

FROM:

RE: KEEPING THE SPIRIT ALIVE

When Sam Walton died, it was business as usual at Wal-Mart. And that's the way Mr. Walton — the man who made customer service an art — wanted it. Will the organization he created continue to be both a boon to shareholders and a benchmark for admirers? Business history is replete with examples of companies that died with their founders because they took on the personality of a single individual rather than developing structural and cultural lives of their own. When one individual's persona becomes what psychologist John Cattell calls the "syntality" of the organization, that organization is in peril. It lacks the structure to exist autonomously. Like a child suddenly cut off from parental nurturing, it can't fend for itself and its chances for survival are bleak.

Similarly, the manager who is too insecure to delegate, who will not free people, who insists on being the star, and who clutches power like a child a security blanket will leave as a legacy just those things and nothing more.

When people come together to achieve a common purpose, an organization is formed. This organization can be large or small, public or private, for profit of not for profit. No matter what the mission, it is people, all kinds of people, who score goals and achieve success. Therefore, the role of a good manager is one of melding goals, structures, and people into accomplishment-attaining vehicles capable of benefiting a wide range of constituencies. Simply stated, management is a long-term process that continually transforms diverse elements into supportive relationships. Good management is not a given. In fact, good management must recognize that employees today have radically altered their demands and their expectations. It is the great organizations like Wal-Mart that recognize these changes and respond accordingly.

MEMORANDUM

TO:

FROM:

RE: THINKING THE UNTHINKABLE

While many organizations are overstaffed and over-leveled (with too many rungs between the top and bottom), overstaffing itself, like employee turnover and absenteeism, is essentially symptomatic rather than causal. It is a direct consequence of the "more is always better" approach. In high-performance organizations, this formula is rarely useful, unless the more refers to productivity, quality, and commitment — not just more people.

What is often required is more thinking — thinking unlimited by what once was, nontraditional and oft-times unconventional approaches to structure and human resource utilization. Survival just might be inextricably bound to developing a management mentality where age-old problems are approached with a combination of an understanding of basics and boundless enthusiasm for the always-elusive better way.

MEMORANDUM

TO:

FROM:

RE: IF YOU PLAN TO DRINK THE PUNCH, DON'T RELIEVE YOURSELF IN THE PUNCHBOWL

A more delicate way of putting that thought is the popular adage, "What goes around, comes around."

Do unto others, and while you are at it, think of the long term. You may need tomorrow the good will of that person you savaged today. Unless you have over-whelming masochistic tendencies, keep your fields of operation and concern clear and clean.

Think for a moment of a pond. It's nearby, and you enjoy fishing there. It's a thing of joy. However, as is often the case, nature is taken for granted and, bit by bit, the pond becomes polluted. The fish die. What was a delight is now a disaster.

Now think of the corporate environment, and of the tendency to do what is convenient there, instead of what is right. Between 1980 and 1990, Eastern Air Lines, the company founded by famous pilot Eddie Rickenbacker, was profitable only one year. Everyone was fighting with everyone else, and in the wake of that struggle, 25,000 people in Florida found them-selves out of work. As others were crashing and burn-ing, Eastern's chairman — former astronaut Frank Borman — descended on a golden parachute in Las Cruces, New Mexico, and opened a car dealership.

MEMORANDUM

TO:

FROM:

**RE: MANAGING THE
NOT-ESPECIALLY MOTIVATED**

You think empowerment theories don't work?

You're right. Much of what is written and taught about bringing forth the best from employees is premised on the assumption that every manager manages a corps of people whose sterling characters, latent brilliance and thwarted drive for excellence are there — somewhere.

Not so. Some people are just not worth a tinker's dam in the workplace. Others regard work for pay as their right, and fie on responsibility. Their failings are always someone else's fault.

But somewhere above this extreme lies the majority of less-than-ideal employees. Here you find the folks who — because of attitude or prior training or innate limitations — need supervision in order to reach that nirvana called "empowerment." Take, for example, students working their way through college. They need the job to make it to graduation; they're usually — though not always — reasonably bright people; they're usually — though not always — disciplined enough to show up for work.

But that's often where it ends. Pity the manager — charged with running the registrar's office or the operations organization or the computer service department — who has to see that the job gets done with workers who are transient, indifferent or vastly diverse in backgrounds and orientations to work.

Here are some suggestions:

■ Realize that your own future rests, in some measure, on how effectively you meet this most difficult challenge. It's still a small world, and what you do now may end up in some organizational grapevine two decades from now.

■ Try to fit the task to the person. If Jane Doe wants to tackle the big job of counting all the widgets in inventory, then let her try. If John Doe can't seem to stick with the task to completion, then give him less intricate work to do.

■ Be there. Understand that your job, when necessary, is to teach people *their* jobs, step by step. Taking such an approach not only assures you that subordinates have been offered good training, but also that they have been informed of your expectations, in no uncertain terms.

■ Be precise. With some people, all you need is to say, "Can you get thus-and-so done by Thursday?" But with others, particularly the unmotivated or the immature, you need to make your expectations (1) clear and (2) simple, so there's no wiggling room.

■ Reward. Praise and encouragement are powerful tools, especially if the accolade has really been earned. Although it's a rare manager of the marginal worker who has the budgetary wherewithal to give people that most meaningful of workplace incentives — money — you can perhaps devise other things that people appreciate.

MEMORANDUM

TO:

FROM:

RE: POLICIES, PROCEDURES, RULES AND REGULATIONS

She was stuck in line at one of the many fast-food restaurants that dot our urban, suburban, and rural landscapes today. The customer was locked in the drive-thru lane. Actually, how often are you truly able to drive through the drive-thru lane? Often the traffic in the drive-thru lane rivals I-75, I-20, I-95, and I-10 combined on a Friday afternoon at 5:07 p.m.

At any rate, the customer was stuck in line on a Saturday morning at this eating emporium, her car wedged between a pickup with oversized tires and a Volkswagen with 14 high-schoolers on their way to the beach. The customer was in line waiting to order a breakfast sandwich for herself and a milkshake for her 18-month-old daughter.

The lines in drive-thru lanes at fast-food restaurants would make the late, great Henry Ford proud. Like many functioning production lines, they allow no room for early exit after you enter the queue. Once you're in, you're in for the duration. Why the fast-food restaurants don't try to capitalize on our captivity and market a host of other commodities, like lube jobs, tire changes, and car washes, is beyond us. But in regard to fast-food, one wonders if the many rapid-meal merchants forgot what their business is all about. Many times, "drive-thru" should probably be changed to "drive-thru — if you can, and at your own risk."

The customer entered the lane at 10:08 a.m. Her turn at the speaker arrived at last. She placed her order and waited for the response. There was silence on the other end. Finally, the young clerk responded, "Ma'am, we don't sell shakes before 10:30." There was silence again. The customer looked at her watch, which now read 10:27, and observed, "It's almost 10:30." The clerk, the front-line representative of that multinational, multibillion-dollar organization, repeated, "We don't sell shakes before 10:30." (Page 227 of the company training manual.) The customer suggested that given the number of cars in front of her, she probably would not reach the window until 10:45 and could they please process the order — her child would be most appreciative. It was a standoff. The customer was trapped and the employee nailed. There were cars in front and cars behind, so the customer calmly stated, "I'll wait here for three more minutes until 10:30 arrives and then place my order." After another silence, the voice on the other end said, "Okay."

This frustrating story is true. It is an occurrence which — though commonplace — would astound the most casual observer and stupefy students of management. Policies, procedures, and rules that strangle organizations — big or small — will prove devastating in the short run and will eventually shut down a business. Providing customers with what they want and when they want it are two constants that should not require repeating. Yet time and time again, cash customers are thwarted by enterprises unready, unwilling, and incapable of accepting money at just the right time.

MEMORANDUM

TO:

FROM:

RE: LEAD BY DEED

It was a 7:00 a.m. undergraduate course. The subject was management. For almost all of the students, it was their first exposure to the subject. The professor, in outlining his policy, indicated that the class would begin at 7:00 a.m. sharp, and tardy students would not be allowed to enter. He further explained that he would repeat this announcement for three straight classes, giving each student an opportunity to weather the shock, adjust, or simply make other arrangements. The professor explained that the class would be studying management, and managers should not expect others to do what they won't or can't do themselves. Simply stated, the manager is a role model whose behavior is watched and often emulated. The manager should lead by deed.

Many students perceived the on-time or no-admittance policy as unfair, improper, un-American or just plain crazy. Some indicated they lived long distances from campus. The professor suggested they leave home earlier. Others stated they were working, or had families with whom to contend. This excuse generated even less sympathy, since the average age of the undergraduate student in the class was 28, and 85 percent worked either full- or part-time.

Still, a few felt compelled to test the on-time or no-admittance policy and were left out, looking in. Some of the younger students had parents call the professor to find out why, if they were paying tuition, their children couldn't enter class whenever they arrived. To these parents, the professor explained not only the nature of the course, but his desire to make certain their children developed a winning and responsible habit. Not one parent contested the policy after that explanation.

Actually, after the first three warnings, not only was tardiness *not* a problem, but attendance was unusually high and very few students dropped the class.

Now, the real shock was the statement by many of the students that this was the very first time they were ever held accountable in this fashion. Remember, 85 percent were employed, and yet promises-kept-and-deadlines-met behavior was not only initially considered off the wall, but out of this world. However, once they understood the rationale, virtually all students showed up and succeeded — further demonstrating that most of us do exactly what we want to do, have time for those things we want to have time for, and remember what we truly consider to be important. Of course, there are factors we can't control. Happily, they seldom affect productivity, quality, and attitudinal issues. When they do, folks are generally both sympathetic and empathetic.

MEMORANDUM

TO:

FROM:

RE: LISTENING INSIDE AND OUT

"The problem is lack of communication." In class-room-case analysis and in the real world, lack of communication is cited as the villain more often than any other problem. In reality, lack of communication is more often symptomatic of factors deeply (and sometimes not so deeply) buried in the organization.

Dr. Keith Davis, a legendary communications guru, argues that one of the greatest obstacles to effective communication is our gross inability to listen . . . to stop talking. Our commitment to effective communication must start with a belief, from the highest levels of the organization, that customers, employees, and suppliers have valuable insights to offer. Davis argues that nature gave people two ears, but only one tongue — a gentle hint that we should listen more than talk. The listening is a confirmation that the people within the firm care about you and your ideas or concerns.

Domino's Pizza has revolutionized the food-delivery business by simply committing itself to the philosophy that each and every customer, regardless of position, status, or standing, will receive his pizza within 30 minutes . . . guaranteed. This simple policy communicates to the public at large that each individual order, with or without anchovies, is important to the health and welfare of the company. This two-way communication sends an important message to everyone coming in contact with the organization: the company listens to its customers.

MEMORANDUM

TO:

FROM:

RE: KEEP THE TRUST

A woman goes into her boss's office to announce that, three days earlier, her fertility doctor had pronounced her pregnant. She thanks her boss profusely for supporting her absences from work during a year of treatment. She and her husband haven't even told either set of in-laws.

A few weeks later, this woman answers the phone one day. It's the boss's wife, who says, "Bob told me you're pregnant. I'm so happy for you."

The baby was lost by spontaneous abortion the weekend before. The would-be mother is pained and embarrassed. But more than that, she's angry.

"I didn't mind telling him," she says later, "because his understanding was what allowed me those endless days off to go through those murderous fertility treatments. But it never occurred to me that he'd tell his wife, who'd feel free to mention it to me.

"I didn't tell my friends or family because I knew I might lose the baby. I told my boss, when his door was closed. He went home and blabbed to his wife, who knows people I see socially. I felt betrayed."

Let that be a lesson for you, managers. You are expected to treat an employee's confidences as would a priest. You tell no one. Otherwise, you lose forever something you can't get back, and that is your trustworthiness.

It is said that a secret is no longer a secret if two people know it. Let's amend that to mean that something can be a secret if two people know it, but it won't remain so if one of them tells a spouse or a trusted lieutenant or the assistant manager. Just because you "trust" some third party does not mean that the person who confided in you does.

MEMORANDUM

TO:

FROM:

RE: THE SMALL ROOM CONCEPT

There's nothing really complex or intricate about the way business should be conducted — particularly in the area of customer relations. Our best advice would be to treat each and every customer as if you had to live with this person in a very small room for the rest of your life. If you follow this rule, the customer will be pleased, you will make a profit and you will add that customer to your sales force at no additional cost to you.

To be more than "okay," to please people, you must create an organizational climate where going above and beyond the call of duty is routine, not exceptional. Merely satisfied customers are not really locked into an organization. Companies that deliver okay products and services have, at best, okay results. In the long term, they become noncompetitive.

On a recent flight to the west coast, an executive from Tupperware anxiously related his whirlwind travel schedule. When asked if he was touring company manufacturing or distribution facilities, he smiled and said no. During the course of the year, he would visit hundreds of gatherings of groups of independent Tupperware representatives to thank them for a job well done. "You see," he said, "it is thanks to the efforts of our individual, independent representatives that millions of Americans know that our products 'burp.' And that reflection of our product's consistency and quality, that release of air indicating that our container is indeed airtight, is done on a person-to-person, seller-to-buyer level. It is my job to simply say thank you."

Let people inside and out know you truly appreciate a job well done. Tell them privately and publicly. Don't ever take anything for granted.

MEMORANDUM

TO:

FROM:

RE: ONE MORE GIANNINI

For the several hundred present, it was a happy occasion. Bank of America had just celebrated an outstanding year, and many of those responsible were at a company meeting. During a question-and-answer session, one of the bank's officers observed that "What we need at Bank of America is one more Giannini." A.P. Giannini was the founder of Bank of Italy, which later became the Bank of America.

When asked why, the officer replied, "When Giannini was here, you knew it. If you did a good job, he told you. If you didn't, he let you know. Giannini was visible and accessible. He was capable of relating to other human beings face to face and person to person. He was able to communicate: 'I know, I understand, I am concerned, and I care.'"

In discussing leadership, this banker was right on target. People who do more than manage and who are able to meld the mechanics of the management process with the dynamics of leadership are indeed visible and accessible. They place a premium on face-to-face, open, and honest interaction. Others know they are truly concerned.

A worldwide view of literally hundreds of organizations confirms that if there is a shortage of anything today, it is indeed a shortage of Gianninis — a dearth of individuals in command positions and leadership roles who are, by design, visible and accessible and who can continually communicate to others, "I know, I understand, I am concerned, and I care."

For want of a better term, it is this "Giannini phenomenon" that transforms the ordinary into the extraordinary, the pedestrian into the elite.

MEMORANDUM

TO:

FROM:

RE: MANAGEMENT BY BLAME

Handling mistakes should be the easiest process in the world. It consists of four things, none of which involves casting around for someone to blame.

- If the damage can be undone, undo it straightaway.
- If it's too late, then converse reasonably with those concerned about what happened and how amends can be made.
- Make sure to identify — and communicate to everyone involved — how the mistake could have been avoided.
- Without further ado, get on about your business.

It's not so much that well-trained, responsible people never make errors. The lesson here is that they are more likely to accept responsibility for their work and improve it if they're allowed to learn from the experience. Otherwise, they just entrench themselves into habits of passing the buck.

If your organization makes people afraid of it, then you quite effectively train them to behave as children do when homework is lost. They lie, deny and blame the dog.

MEMORANDUM

TO:

FROM:

RE: JUST AN IDEA

Recently, giant TRW Corporation, a California-based credit-reporting firm, ran an advertisement in *Fortune* magazine. Its caption read, "It was just an idea." In part, the advertisement read, "An idea is a fragile thing. Turning it off is much easier than keeping it lit . . . Ideas shone because somebody had them and somebody helped them, and nobody turned them off."

How did you respond the last time somebody had a wild and crazy idea?

MEMORANDUM

TO:

FROM:

RE: KINDLING LIGHTS FIRES, BUT
COALS MAKE THEM BURN.

Don't misunderstand. We like hotshots. They're the
corporate wunderkind, whether they're green whip-
persnappers with more book-learning than sense, or
sage troopers secure in their experience. They're the
live wires whose vigor provides companies with energy and innovation. They've set many a staid corporation or languid department on its tail, with results
that were all to the good.

Sometimes that's all they do — come in with a rush,
make some impressive cosmetic changes, and leave
with little — in the end — to show for their tenure.
These are the ones who are hotshots but nothing
more. Like false prophets, they present themselves
well to top management and charm it into giving
them responsible jobs. Coworkers despise them.

Other live wires, though, have the ability to vitalize
organizations for years, and to earn colleagues'
esteem.

You want to attract — and keep — the latter. To do
that, your organization must offer a framework that
not only welcomes hotshots, but also ripens them to
maturity. It's one thing to start a fire. It's quite anoth-

er to keep it going. Here are a few suggestions:

■ Don't insult a hotshot's programs before time has told whether or not they are going to be successful. Similarly, don't prematurely celebrate hotshots for superficial accomplishments.

■ Don't allow a hotshot to run wild. If you want to see how he or she is doing in the organization, talk to the people in it — the people who report to the individual and those who provide his or her support services.

■ Let the hotshot know, in no uncertain terms, that you define a good manager as someone who — however deftly he or she brings in the profits — can also get along with other people, earn their respect and treat them fairly.

MEMORANDUM

TO:

FROM:

RE: IT'S A MUDDLE, ALL RIGHT.

The reason traditional evaluations defeat their own purpose is that the employee doesn't know until the end of a year what he or she has been evaluated for. Expectations change, unaccountably, in the interim. If Joe's last evaluation said, "Get to the point in your reports," and he has cut out a lot of verbiage, then this year's evaluation can suggest, "Don't do so-and-so, or try to improve this and that." The hapless employee didn't even know this or that had become a problem.

Well, it's a problem now, because something someone didn't even know he or she was doing or not doing is now on the permanent record.

Is this effective — or fair? Is it the best way for American companies to elicit the most productive behavior from their workers?

MEMORANDUM

TO:

FROM:

RE: VALIDATION IS . . .

Validation means confirming what something is, or vouching for what someone does. When done correctly by managers, validation is immeasurably valuable to employees. The process is one of holding up mirrors in a room of soft lights. The mirrors allow people to view strengths and weaknesses; the soft lights remove harshness from the panorama.

Validation involves listening and conversing, not pontificating and lecturing. It evokes honesty and clarity, not subterfuge and confusing messages. It suggests concentrating on the possible rather than pandering to the impossible. Managers who validate their employees don't imply to someone with limited ability that he or she can run the bank.

MEMORANDUM

TO:

FROM:

RE: RESISTANCE TO CHANGE

At a recent meeting of federal executives, an issue arose regarding the use of suggestion systems in order to collect insights and ideas from employees. The regional manager proudly stood and said his group did indeed have such a document that served his 10,000 civil servants exceptionally well. When asked whether he could produce the document, he replied, "Absolutely." He then presented a beautifully bound "suggestion system policies and procedures guide." Did the system also include financial rewards for innovative cost savings or revenue enhancing ideas? Certainly. The next logical question was, of course, how much money was distributed the previous year for world-beating suggestions? The reply: none. The question was rephrased: how many suggestions did these 10,000 employees offer the previous year. The answer: none.

Something was not right. A great-looking manual, a firm set of policies and procedures in place, and no ideas to show for it. Why not? The collective response was simply that the system was just too complicated. You see, form, not function, ruled that organization, and change was totally inhibited. No suggestions, no problems.

We have both overt and subtle ways of resisting change, and these are communicated and understood quite clearly. The strongest resistance to change generally comes from those who don't understand the process. Resistance to change becomes a badge of arrogance that is unhealthy and counterproductive. How do you encourage, foster and incubate change in your organization?

MEMORANDUM

TO:

FROM:

RE: LEADER/MANAGER

While those with managerial titles abound, world-class manager/leaders are aberrations, and watching them in operation can be a thrilling event. Here is a list of characteristics which might help in differentiating the winners from the also-rans:

■ The leader/manager helps develop a wish-you-well culture. As you know, in many organizations, people wish you well, but wish themselves better. The leader/manager creates a climate where we can enjoy and celebrate the success of others as we would our own achievements.

■ The leader/manager is neither paternalistic nor maternalistic. After all, the mantle of leadership does not necessarily imply you know what's best for other people.

■ The leader/manager is secure enough to understand that to err is human, to forgive, downright unusual. He or she does not collect real or imaginary injustices.

■ The leader/manager understands the power of openness and shared knowledge. People who understand the "why" have a much better opportunity of contributing and succeeding.

■ The leader/manager can conceptualize, understand how all the pieces fit, and is capable of melding the three critical elements of goals, structure, and people.

Certainly, these qualities only scratch the surface. However, they might serve as a handy guide for spotting those who truly lead by movement — not mouth.

MEMORANDUM

TO:

FROM:

**RE: VISION AND MISSION
TRANSFORMATION:
PARTICIPATION, PLEASE**

There's absolutely no doubt about it. We are drowning in vision and mission statements.

Exquisitely crafted and elegantly framed, they proclaim the good intentions and lofty standards of major and not-so-major organizations. Unfortunately, in all too many instances, these statements belong to a small group of folks who were involved in developing and writing them. Hence, more often than not, there is absolutely no sense of ownership among those who are supposed to transform vision and mission into realities.

If you want consensus in implementation, it is only appropriate that opportunities for involvement are provided in the developmental stages.

This does not mean that everyone will want to participate, but it does assure that all have at least been given the chance. Simply opening up the process will work wonders.

Having completed 26 million square feet of office space, 15,000 hotel rooms, and seven million square feet of retail facilities in almost half the states in this country, the Hardin Company has some unique operational insights into organizational mentality, along with an incessant and obsessive attention to detail. In its 45-year history, Hardin has built a great organization with great management and greater employees. Site managers/superintendents have the explicit authority to deliver . . . period. The objective: a zero punch list yielding fewer problems and frustrations and more repeat business from a loyal customer base.

Company philosophy drives this winning organization and the attention-to-detail ethic has served the firm well. Of the ten-point philosophy statement, five are reflective of a passionate belief in focusing on results, shifting accountability and responsibility to the lowest possible levels, a feel-good phenomenon, and the desire to establish a unique corporate culture. The points include:

1. Be a client-driven, proactive business.
2. Insist on open and honest communications in all directions.
3. Build a lean management team that exhibits visible and effective leadership through example.
4. Attract, orient, develop, educate, motivate, and effectively utilize a professional workforce.
5. Assume a leadership role in the communities we serve and participate in community philanthropic efforts.

These beliefs and the ability to transform thoughts into deeds have moved Hardin into the ranks of the 50 largest construction-management firms . . . simple, elegant, and profitable.

MEMORANDUM

TO:

FROM:

**RE: ON COMMANDING,
    DEMANDING AND CRYING WOLF**

Effective managers usually don't command, and almost never demand. The rigid, authoritarian structures that long nurtured the militaristic executive have been tested and found wanting. This isn't to say that managers no longer have any right whatever to say, "Yours is not to reason why" to a subordinate — when there's a fire, you move. There will be ample time after the crisis for discussion. For now, clear the building.

Some managers, however, are always seeing fires. These individuals operate on an everything-is-an-emergency basis. They've raised crying wolf to such a high art that the workplaces they control have becomes museums of mass hysteria. People like this neither manage nor lead. They merely react — and overreact. Because their view of reality is so narrow, so governed by mindless anticipation of the worst, they attempt to control the self-created chaos by commanding and demanding. These are immensely destructive people. No matter how brilliant, they are invariably detrimental to the health and well-being of any endeavor.

Contrast the cry-wolf, command-and-demand style

with that of the manager-leader who helps create a climate in which the desire to be part of an organization is so strong that people achieve things that no amount of browbeating could make them achieve. In such an organization, the demands placed on the individual by the individual are far greater than anything dreamed up by a brow-beater or a nervous nelly.

Is it easy to build this kind of organization? Never. Is such an organization usually profitable? Always.

MEMORANDUM

TO:

FROM:

**RE: IF ONLY THEY WOULD
    STRAIGHTEN UP**

Executives who year after year march an endless
stream of consultants through the work areas and
conference rooms are not unlike parents who march
their children to a new psychiatrist every year. The
message is, "I am fine. Now you do something about
them."

MEMORANDUM

TO:

FROM:

RE: GROW ANOTHER EAR

Most of us walk about with the standard issue of two ears. The best and most effective managers have at least three. It is the third ear that really makes the difference, observed psychologist and former management professor Dr. G. Hugh Russell.

1. With ear number one, listen to what the other person says. If some people just did this much, they'd already be well ahead of the pack.
2. With ear number two, listen to what the other person *wants* to say, since what he or she does not express can be much more important than what is actually vocalized.
3. With the third ear, you try to hear what the other person means to say but simply does not know how.

Then, why not lean forward, smile, and help the struggling soul along? The consummate manager/leader develops that third-ear sensitivity to the point where others feel free and comfortable and able to talk and communicate. In the process, a better manager emerges, along with a more relaxed, productive worker.

MEMORANDUM

TO:

FROM:

RE: IT STARTS AT THE TOP

Good customer relations begin with sound staff relations, and the genesis of sound staff relations is at
the top. Chances are, the treatment you receive as a
customer is precisely the treatment the clerk is
receiving from the boss.

No single company has "grown it the right way" better than Home Depot. Other retailers have captured
the public's fancy during the past decade, including
Wal-Mart, Nordstrom, Toys "R" Us, and the Price
Club, but none has grown it any better than Home
Depot. Today, this $5 billion do-it-yourself, home-
repair chain is the largest in the United States. While
the company's stores are primarily located in the
Sunbelt, Arthur Blank and Bernard Marcus, the
founding and guiding gurus of Home Depot, expect
to have more than 350 stores throughout the U.S. by
1995. In 11 truly spectacular years, Blank and Marcus
have demonstrated that there is a method to their
madness. Almost every employee receives four weeks
of training before a store opening, and storewide
start-up training costs approach half a million dollars. The stores are immense (30,000 items), and
prices are great (33 percent below typical retail
prices), but the greatness of Home Depot is predicat-
ed on developing a world-class sales team that can

move immense amounts of merchandise.

It is the salesperson at the store level who has helped this company grow to a preeminent position in the industry. This is top-to-bottom management at work.

MEMORANDUM

TO:

FROM:

RE: EVERYONE DOES WINDOWS

One day, Anthony Burns, the CEO of Ryder System, a multibillion-dollar truck leasing organization in Miami, Florida, was entering corporate headquarters. The executive veered from the main entry path, strolled onto the immaculately manicured front lawn and picked up a candy wrapper. When asked why not let the groundskeepers take care of it, Mr. Burns had a simple response. He said that the sign of a quality organization is symbolic. It is cleanliness, having products face buyers with the names clearly visible, greeting customers with a smile and simply saying thank you. To Mr. Burns, this is the goal of Ryder System. It is the goal of the company but more importantly, of the people who make up the company — including its top executives.

MEMORANDUM

TO:

FROM:

RE: A FAMILY AFFAIR

So, should you go into a family business? A fair question and one that's often asked. Generally, the idea has merit, but only if you are a member of the family. Admittedly, there are some notable exceptions, but when the moment of truth comes, and it always does, blood is thicker than water, and a son, daughter, or recently acquired in-law might get the nod. Forget merit and seniority; we're talking reality and kinship.

Too often, we've seen the non-family member excluded when it comes time to divide the spoils and watched bonuses paid to family members whose major contribution is that they stay away. Some contend this is the golden rule in action. Not the sound, do-unto-others Golden Rule, but the one that recognizes those with the gold rule and those with equity tied to birth are far more equal than a productive non-family member.

If you opt for the family concern, either be a family member or have a safety net. Don't say we didn't warn you.

MEMORANDUM

TO:

FROM:

RE: NO MORE CATALYSTS

At a recent meeting of company presidents, a speaker exhorted each CEO to be a "catalyst." He wasn't a very good speaker, and he gave old advice that is as inappropriate today as it ever was.

Actually, we need far less of this catalytic thinking.

When you function as a catalyst, you can change the behavior of others without in any way at all affecting your own. What's needed are more change agents who not only are capable of altering the behavior of others, but who are willing and able to change themselves first.

Who doesn't love a parade? Parade-watching can be exciting, enjoyable, and entertaining. With a seat in the first row, it can be downright thrilling. However, put a parade-watcher in charge and the result is a spectacle of another variety. As he clings to the past and present, the only movement emanating from the parade-watcher is one of treading water. Generally, the parade-watcher is so busy staying afloat or marking time that he or she neglects what must be done — and sooner than one might imagine, the organization becomes an artifact and the parade-watcher a fossil.

John Sherman, previously a megacommercial developer in Kentucky and up until recently mayor of upscale Bal Harbour, Florida, was sick and tired of too many parade-watchers and not enough change-makers . . . of too much mouth and not enough movement. Specifically, Sherman was troubled by the moribund response to the idea of helping bright, deserving, but underfinanced kids go to college. His answer: a special scholarship endowment fund, seeded with his own capital, to guarantee financial support to outstanding graduates of elementary schools upon successful completion of high school five years later. The incentive had to be provided early in the process. Sherman, counting the number of parade-watchers, assumed the role of drum major, of changemaker, and got the parade moving.

Change can only be managed when management itself has the desire and the willingness to do what must be done.

MEMORANDUM

TO:

FROM:

RE: OUNCES OF PREVENTION

Turn off of Memorial Drive — garishly cluttered by
fast-food chains, car lots and middlebrow strips — in
Stone Mountain, Georgia, and you arrive at Gordon
Bailey Advertising. There, on a relatively quiet street,
it's not uncommon to see cars parked around the two
Georgian buildings at any hour and on almost any day.

Is this immensely successful business-to-business
agency a sweatshop? Not hardly. Some of the 43
employees have been with the company since its
1972 beginnings in Mr. Bailey's garage. Whether
they're go-go salespeople or dreamier creative souls,
they work the way they do because that is how they
enjoy using their many skills. And because these
people can also earn the right to share in company
profits, some of them will probably be millionaires by
the time they retire.

Are these folks driven? Someone who takes a more
laid-back approach might look at Bailey-ites and say
"definitely." However, there are no time clocks at Gordon Bailey Advertising. The authoritative word here is
"choice."

Not all companies operate like this one, nor should
they. In some, people work 20 to 40 hours a week,

depending on how their assigned tasks fill the organization's needs and their own. In other cases, people
work only nine, ten or eleven months of the
 year. These people, in these firms, still enjoy fulfill-
ing work lives and still perform stunningly for their
employers.

The point is not whether or not some company is a
"sweatshop" or a "bed of roses." The point is that its
leadership knows how to hire.

Gordon Bailey's hiring process is extraordinary. While
not designed to be intimidating or unpleasant, it is
nonetheless meticulous. But more important than
the mechanics of how this company decides which
people to take on is the fact that it does not engage
people who — regardless of their skills and experience and other paper qualifications — don't share its
particular work ethic.

It's the idea that an ounce of prevention is worth a
pound of cure.

MEMORANDUM

TO:

FROM:

RE: SHOP YOUR OWN BUSINESS

In the moving and thought-provoking movie *The Doctor*, the gifted William Hurt portrays a caustic and callous surgeon who finds himself with a cancerous tumor in his throat. The movie captures his transformation from an unfeeling, uncaring, insensitive, boorish surgeon to one who truly empathizes with his patients. From a business perspective, there is a wonderful lesson in this for all of us: shop your own business.

Rarely, if ever, do we take the time to shop our own establishments. We focus our energies and efforts on a daily basis upon managing and crisis control. But like Hurt's experience in *The Doctor*, it would benefit all of us to become one of our own customers.

Hurt is rudely alerted to the stark, impersonality of his own hospital — forms to complete, waiting for hours on end, unanswered questions. For "the customer" it adds up to a humiliating experience. Hurt's metamorphosis is one that all of us might experience if we took the time and effort to buy from ourselves.

Simple things, such as telephone etiquette, waiting time, product/service availability, product knowledge, promptness of service and courtesy, would be scrutinized much more carefully and on a much more regular basis if we bothered to patronize our businesses. Indeed, calling your own office can provide many an insight into the level of your operation where buyers meet sellers. Front-line transactions in each of our enterprises, public or private, large or small, constitute the level where deals are done. And yet, rarely, if ever, do we take the time, energy and effort to examine operations on the line, on a regularly scheduled basis. What Hurt learned is what all of us should know. Empathy, warmth, a sense of humor and honesty contribute to the effectiveness of our businesses. What's generally lacking, though, is the constant training and reinforcement so desperately needed at the front line to emphasize how important these attributes are.

MEMORANDUM

TO:

FROM:

RE: ON COLLECTING INJUSTICES

Whether it's a paper cup or Baccarat crystal, the vessel some people hold is always half-empty. These individuals have a penchant for the negative that, while not life-threatening, is downright unbearable for those who have to work with them. Nothing produced is good enough, fault-finding is taken to absurd extremes, and praise is found only in the dictionary.

The possibility of such managers building winning teams is remote. Subordinates focus their energies on maintaining enough sanity to function until other employment can be found.

In other cases, employees come to behave the way they think the manager expects them to behave, and the boss's negativism is intensified and multiplied to ruinous extremes. A collection of people who should be functioning as a unit becomes engaged in intra-mural warfare. Eventually, the adversarial atmosphere spreads to customers, vendors, family members and anyone else who happens to breathe its air.

Rabbi Harry Epstein, an outstanding theologian who lives in Atlanta, once delivered a memorable sermon about injustice collectors. They are the folks who focus on the negative, who pick your bones for real and imaginary wrongs and — once found— gather those transgressions with the fervor of IRS agents.

The half-empty manager is an injustice collector. If you see one coming, run — don't walk. If you work for one, look for another job. Life's far too short.

MEMORANDUM

TO:

FROM:

RE: THE CLASS-ACT MANAGER

He said, "Hello."

Absolutely unbelievable. Ben Gilmer answered his phone that day, just like a real person.

He was being telephoned for a bit of advice, but the caller had been certain beforehand that reaching Mr. Gilmer would be virtually impossible. It would involve dozens of please-holds and state-your-business queries. None of that happened. The number was dialed and the phone answered by a courteous, attentive and interested human being who also happened to be the CEO of AT&T, one or the world's largest corporations.

Although the call took place many years ago, the lesson is current. The class-act manager, whenever possible, makes certain that he or she is approachable — that people from any of the company's constituencies have a chance to interact with the big boss.

Maintaining this kind of sensitivity is precisely what must be evident at the top of any organization. When it is, the good will cascades downward and outward until it engulfs every single person. Only when that happens does the company begin to generate loyalty, commitment, productivity, quality and all the other things that yield success and profitability.

Just think. It all starts with something small, like a phone call.

MEMORANDUM

TO:

FROM:

RE: REMEMBER YOUR ROOTS

The late Alex Haley probably did more to emphasize the importance of roots than anyone else in the past few decades. While recollecting origins with humility and honesty is good for the individual, it is absolutely essential for an organization that has arrived and may be becoming complacent.

Take, for example, IBM. Many years ago, at the company's Homestead facility in Endicott, New York, and elsewhere, the "Big Blue" designation was a real accolade. Although IBM might have had an unwritten, uniform-of-the-day policy that tended to quash individual differences, its market triumphs were anything but stereotypical. The company had a mystique that permeated the entire organization and positively affected customers and vendors alike. IBM service was a hallmark, a standard to which others aspired and against which they were measured. And when the IBM Glee Club at Homestead performed, singers didn't regard their tunes as corny or hokey; these folks actually believed everything they were singing about, and they were singing about their company.

It's still their company. But there are now many thousands fewer of them. What happened to Big Blue? Many things, some of which were beyond its control.

But one was that IBM's toughest competition was not beating at its walls from outside; it was growing right within its framework.

The instant you forget how you got to be as good as you are, you become just like everyone else.

MEMORANDUM

TO:

FROM:

RE: BEYOND THE GOLDEN RULE

A group of men stands around in the office, all riveted to the one bragging loudly about a recent sexual encounter. When a woman, who is sitting within earshot, turns and glares at them, they laugh sheepishly and shamble off.

One worker calls people "nigger" or "seaweed eater" and, when taken to task, gets off the hook with a blasé "Whatsamatter? Can't you take a joke?"

A female employee can't seem to refrain from dropping hints about her fondness for being unclothed in the presence of men.

The task force on diversity urges people to be sensitive and respectful.

Get real, companies. Forget committees. The workplace is not the proper forum for discussing what is done to, for or by people's bodies, any more than it is the place for airing personal prejudices. Make a policy that says so and fire those who show no respect for it, with no ifs, ands or buts.

MEMORANDUM

TO:

FROM:

RE: DEVELOPERS OR DEVELOPEES?

Once it smiles on individuals and promotes them, Amalgamated Amalgamation's executive suite goes blithely about its business and watches for results. It rarely does one thing it needs to do, which is check up on how well those managers are faring with their subordinates. And it never, never seems to do the other thing it needs to do, which is respect those subordinates enough to ask them how they are faring under the new bosses.

No one has yet invented the manager's job that, by itself and left unattended, will make an insecure person secure or a real jerk into a decent manager.

One reason rank-and-filers grumble bitterly about the executive suite is that its inhabitants throw into management people who haven't the remotest notion that being a "manager" means more than
- Making more money
- Telling people what to do
- Acquitting themselves well in meetings with executives.

INDEX

QUALITIES OF GOOD LEADERSHIP

WORKPLACE WISDOM — MISCELLANEOUS MEMOS